BOND MARKET RULES

BOND MARKET RULES

50 Investing Axioms to Master Bonds for Income or Trading

MICHAEL D. SHEIMO

McGraw-Hill

New York San Francisco Washington, D.C. Auckland Bogotá
Caracas Lisbon London Madrid Mexico City Milan
Montreal New Delhi San Juan Singapore
Sydney Tokyo Toronto

Library of Congress Cataloging-in-Publication Data

Sheimo, Michael D., date.
   Bond market rules : 50 investing axioms to master bonds for income
or trading / by Michael D. Sheimo.
     p. cm.
    ISBN 0-07-134860-3
    1. Bonds. I. Title.
HG4651.S466 1999
332.63'23—dc21   99-27456
                                              CIP

McGraw-Hill

*A Division of The **McGraw·Hill** Companies*

Copyright © 2000 by The McGraw-Hill Companies, Inc. All rights reserved. Printed in the United States of America. Except as permitted under the United States Copyright Act of 1976, no part of this publication may be reproduced or distributed in any form or by any means, or stored in a database or retrieval system, without the prior written permission of the publisher.

1 2 3 4 5 6 7 8 9 0 DOC/DOC 9 0 9 8 7 6 5 4 3 2 1 0 9

ISBN 0-07-134860-3

The sponsoring editor for this book was Kelli Christiansen, the editing supervisor was Donna Muscatello, and the production supervisor was Elizabeth J. Strange. It was set in Palatino by Jan Fisher through the services of Barry E. Brown (Broker—Editing, Design and Production).

Printed and bound by R.R. Donnelley & Sons Company.

This publication is designed to provide accurate and authoriative information in regard to the subject matter covered. It is sold with the understanding that neither the author nor the publisher is engaged in rendering legal, accounting, or other professional services. If legal advice or other expert assistance is required, the services of a competent professional person should be sought.

> *—From a Declaration of Principles jointly adopted by a Committee of the American Bar Association and a Committee of Publishers.*

McGraw-Hill books are available at special quantity discounts to use as premiums and sales promotions, or for use in corporate training programs. For more information, please write to the Director of Special Sales, McGraw-Hill, 11 West 19th Street, New York, NY 10011. Or contact your local bookstore.

 This book is printed on recycled, acid-free paper containing a minimum of 50% recycled de-inked fiber.

For Linda,
the bond of my life.

CONTENTS

PREFACE

Short chapters based on single concepts, it's the same approach that worked so well in *Stock Market Rules*, a popular guide on stock investing since 1990. This is a great book to read during lunch.

Bond Market Rules is for beginning- to intermediate-level investors who want to learn or review the basics of investing in bonds. Prices, price action, interest-rate analysis, fundamental and technical analysis, new types of bonds (Bradys, DANs, TIPS), tax-exempt bonds, bonds that increase in face value with inflation, bonds that have a "survivors' put option": all are explained and examined. Bonds have changed. They aren't your father's "bearer bonds" anymore, hidden in the basement.

NEW BENEFITS

Although bonds are not the simple investment they once were, many of the newer innovations benefit the investor. Even an old standard, the T-bill, has changed from a $10,000 to a $1000 minimum investment, thereby making it available to a larger group of investors.

Brady bonds from developing countries have enabled investors to take advantage of higher foreign yields without extreme risk (Chapter 49).

Direct access notes (DANs), offer the income flexibility of six-month or monthly payments on bonds, which can be put back to the company at face value by the investor's estate (Chapter 31). That can be a terrific advantage if interest rates have risen and the heirs have bills to pay.

Even the U.S. government is trying to be accommodating to the investor's concerns. Inflation can be the enemy of fixed-income investing. Rising to this concern are inflation protection bonds (TIPs). When are they a bargain and when are regular bonds better (Chapter 24)?

STRATEGIES

Income, asset allocation, and defensive investing are just some of the concepts examined. Strategies like the "ladder" (Chapter 16) make a wonderful inflation hedge when interest rates rise. A simpler version of the ladder is the "barbell," which combines some of the advantages of both short-term and long-term bond investing (Chapter 29). Easier yet are the Treasury Inflation Protection bonds (TIPs), which are tied to the Consumer Price Index. But how much does that "protection" cost?

Asset allocation is explored in Chapter 21. What is meant by allocation? How is it done? What are some variations? The information presented can enable the investor to choose between an approach suitable for profits and one suitable for defensive investing.

ANALYSIS

Always check the yield curve before buying bonds (Chapters 3 and 4). Checking the yield curve will instantly let you know if the long-term yields are worth the holding period. The curve can also give signals as to what might happen next with interest rates. Bond and bond market analyses are discussed in several chapters. Chapters 3, 4, 7, 8, 20, 30, and others contain analysis—from the uncomplicated to the detailed.

BOND FUTURES AND OPTIONS

Options trading can be speculative or conservative, and some of the details are examined in Chapter 16. Although not appropriate for every investor, some basics of bond futures, hedging, and speculating are explored in Chapter 23.

DATA

Unless otherwise noted, the data used in this work comes from the Federal Reserve Bank of St. Louis. Much of their data originates from the Bureau of Labor Statistics. Both of these sources are available on the Internet.

THE INTERNET

It's almost as if the Internet was designed for investors. Hundreds of thousands of pages of economic data and investing information are now available to individuals. Until the Internet came along, much of this information was only available to institutional investors. Now the individual can access the information for analysis and strategic planning.

The only caution with Internet pages is to always look for a date showing when the page was created and the source of the data. Many times pages look new, but are outdated. Several Internet information sources are cited throughout the book.

BOND LANGUAGE

Chapter 50, Learn the Language of Bonds, is an extensive glossary that will help you become familiar with some of the terminology of bond investing. Some of the terms and concepts have endured for decades; some are of very recent origin.

SUITED TO YOUR OBJECTIVES

No matter what your investment objectives are, *Bond Market Rules* can help you plan and organize the bond portion of your portfolio. This book will give you an understanding of what a bond is and how the different types of bonds function. The understanding can make you a better-informed, more prudent, and more profitable investor.

CHAPTER 1

When Interest Rates Rise, Bond Prices Fall

Think about it. If an investor has a bond paying interest of $100 (10%) annually and wants to sell that bond, but similar bonds are now paying out $80 (8%) annual interest, won't that investor want something extra for the more valuable bond? Of course. Therefore a buyer must be willing to pay extra for the higher-interest-rate bond.

Looking at the opposite viewpoint, say an investor has a bond paying $70 (7%) annually and wants to sell, but now similar bonds are paying $100 (10%). In order to get someone to buy that 7% bond, the investor must be willing to accept a lower price. That's why interest rates and bond prices move in opposite directions, like a teeter-totter on a playground with bond prices on one end and interest rates on the other. In effect, bond prices are adjusted to better equalize different bond interest rates. The resulting investment return is generally referred to as *yield*, or *current yield*.

WHAT IS A BOND?

In the world of investing, a bond is a $1000 loan to a company, government, or other organization. Although bond investing abounds with both legalese and trading jargon, a bond is still just a simple loan from an individual to one of the entities mentioned.

An amount of money is loaned to an organization and interest is paid. The proof of the loan and its amount is the investment in-

strument known as a *bond*. Bonds can be bought and sold in a manner similar to, but not quite the same as, stocks.

BUYING BONDS

Except in individual retirement accounts (IRAs), which have limited contributions, many investors buy bonds in quantities of five.
That's $5000 face value (also called par value). *Face value* is the
amount returned or paid to the investor when the bond matures.
Bonds normally exist for a specific number of years (2, 3, 5, 10, 30,
and so on). When the time expires the loan is paid back to the current bondowner. Most bonds have a set interest rate (e.g., 5%, 6%,
7.25%) once the legal bond is established. Since the interest rate on
the bond cannot be changed, the price (stated as a percentage of the
face value) is raised or lowered depending on market interest-rate
changes. Since bonds can be traded, that is, bought and sold, their
prices are adjusted to make the investment competitive with current interest rates. That means a 5% bond could effectively pay
4.5% or 6.5% as its price is raised or lowered.

PRICE AND COUPON

Although there are other considerations in bond pricing (commissions, markups, markdowns, etc.), a move of 10 dollars in price
will cause the yield to move a percentage point. Bond traders measure the move in basis points. One basis point is equal to 1/100 of
a percentage point, therefore a 1% move is 100 basis points.

An example of a hundred basis point move, assuming the same
bond is currently issuing at 7%, a 6% coupon bond would be priced
at 990 dollars. Since the price is normally stated as a percentage of
the thousand-dollar face value, the bond would be at 99. Likewise, a
7% coupon bond presently issuing at 6% is said to be at 101. By ad-
justing the price of the bond, the yield can be made comparable to
current bond issues and the bond can be bought and sold.

CHANGES IN INTEREST RATES

Many individuals think of interest rates as being set at certain levels
that are occasionally readjusted. In reality, interest rates are both set
and fluid, depending on what level is being observed. Essentially,

interest rates begin with the *federal discount rate*. This is set by the Federal Reserve Bank and is changed on an "as needed" basis.

Banks are required to maintain minimum overnight reserves. These reserves can be borrowed from the Federal Reserve Bank at the discount rate. Reserves can also be borrowed from other banks at the *federal-funds rate*. These two rates essentially become the basis for all interest charged to banking customers. They represent a bank's costs. Obviously, interest rates to customers will have to be higher.

THE FEDERAL DISCOUNT RATE

The discount rate works like the accelerator and brakes on a car. If the economy is moving too slowly, the Fed can step on the accelerator by lowering the federal discount rate. This action makes money more available at lower interest rates. If the economy is moving too fast and inflation becomes a threat, the Fed raises interest rates. This makes money less available and more expensive to borrow. Actions taken on the federal discount rate impact the federal-funds rate and prime rate.

A 20-year view of the federal discount rate (Figure 1–1) shows that it is more of a fixed rate that is changed periodically, than one that is constantly changing. Although there is no limit on when or how often the discount rate can be changed, it typically changes only a few times a year. When compared to 30-year bond yields, the relationship between the two becomes readily apparent.

DISCOUNT RATE AND BOND YIELDS

The discount rate and the 30-year bond yield do track each other. Sometimes, as in the early 1980s, the two can be quite close together. This period also saw an inverted yield curve, with short-term interest rates higher than long-term rates (see Chapter 4 and Chapter 5 regarding yield curves). At other times, the difference is much wider, as was the case in 1993.

Notice that changes in the federal discount rate tend to precede changes in the 30-year bond yields when interest rates are falling, but the bond yield changes lead when interest rates are rising (Figure 1–2). A notable exception to this tendency appeared in the late 1970s when the yield curve inverted and short-term rates exceeded long-term interest rates (see Chapter 5). Here, the federal

FIGURE 1–1

Federal Discount Rate 1978–1998

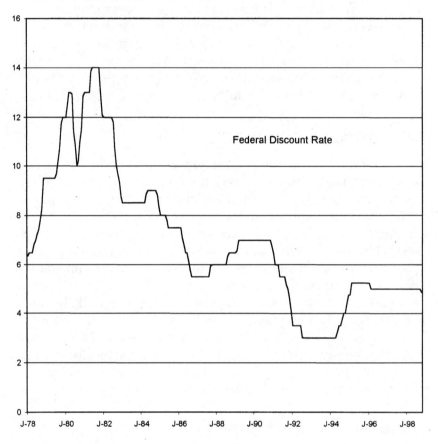

discount rate led the way. The intent was to slow economic advancement by raising interest rates. Once the economic objective was accomplished, the discount rate began to drop (in late 1981), resuming its pattern of leading the 30-year bond yield.

Changes in the federal discount rate cause considerable repercussions. When it changes, one can assume other interest rates, both short- and long-term will follow.

FEDERAL FUNDS RATE

The term *federal-funds rate,* or "fed-funds," as it is commonly called, refers to money that banks can borrow from each other (instead of the Fed) to meet their overnight reserve requirements. Although

FIGURE 1–2

Federal Discount Rate vs. 30 Year 1979–1998

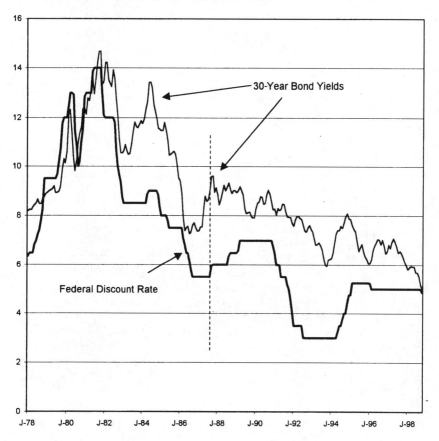

strictly speaking, the Federal Reserve Bank does not control the fed-funds rate, it can have a strong influence on changes. For example, a statement like the following Fed announcement can be enough.

Citing "unusual strains" on financial markets, Federal Reserve policymakers cut interest rates Tuesday, moving for the third time in seven weeks to keep the U.S. economy from slipping into a recession. The Fed announced that it trimmed its target for the federal-funds rate by one-quarter of a percentage point to 4.75%.[1]

1 "Fed Trims Short-Term Interest Rates, Marking Third Cut in Seven Weeks," *Interactive Journal* News Roundup, November 17, 1998, *The Wall Street Journal*, http:// public.wsj.com/news/hmc/sb911314106193166000.htm.

FIGURE 1–3

Fed Funds Rate 1978–1998

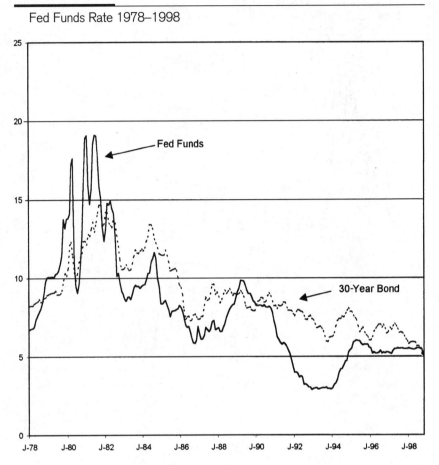

This change was the third since September 29, 1998. At times, influencing the fed-funds rate accomplishes enough by itself. At other times, the federal discount rate is also lowered to strengthen the impact. Here, the discount rate was cut to 4.5% from its previous level of 4.75% (Figure 1–3). Prime lending rates also dropped a quarter of a percent.

PRIME RATE

Prime rate is a familiar term to most people. Essentially, it is the interest rate charged by commercial banks to their best customers (usually corporate customers, not individuals). It is also a base for

FIGURE 1–4

Prime Rate 1978–1998

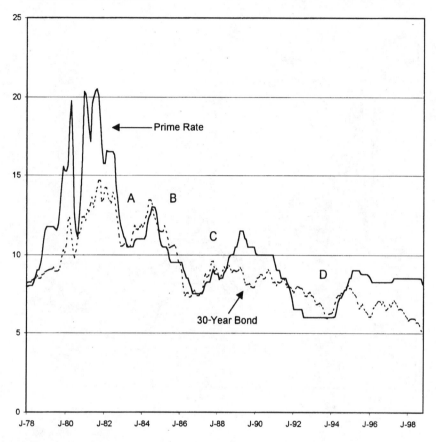

consumer-oriented lending rates. Expressions like "prime plus one and a quarter" or "prime plus three" might be encountered when an individual applies for a bank loan.

Notice in Figure 1–4, the volatility in prime rate in the late seventies and early eighties, similar to other, related interest rates. Also, notice how at points A, B, C, and D, the long-bond interest rate is higher than the prime rate.

THREE INTEREST RATES

Looking at all three rates—discount, funds, and prime—on the same graph illustrates their relationship (Figure 1–5). Most of the

FIGURE 1–5

Three Rates and 30-Year Bond Yields 1978–1998

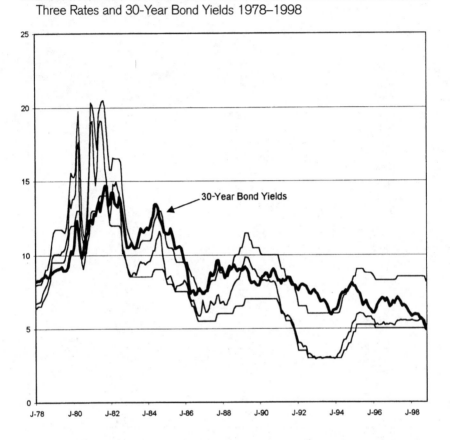

time, the federal discount rate is the lowest, the fed-funds rate appears in the middle, and the prime rate is the highest. Their tendency is to move in concert; as one increases, so do the others. When a decline occurs, it tends to be across-the-board. The disparity between rates varies too, sometimes greater, sometimes less. When the three rates decrease, the economy expands until inflation or the threat of inflation appears. To control or halt inflation, rates are increased as part of a strategy to make money less available.

A comparison between the federal discount rate, fed-funds rate, prime rate, and the 30-year treasury bond rate shows other interesting tendencies. The bold line in Figure 1-5 tracks the yield on the 30-year. As interest rates rise, the yield on the 30-year tends to precede, rising before the other three (exception in the late 1970s with an inverted yield curve). Bond yields rise due to a lack of buyers. If interest rates are going up, few investors are willing to buy the long bond. When there are fewer buyers, prices fall, therefore yields rise, that is why the 30-year yield rises before others. As bond buyers anticipate lower rates, they begin to lock in longerterm bonds by buying the 30-year treasury. The buying action pushes prices higher and yields lower. Also, there is buyer hesitancy with the riskier long-bond, because it's difficult to be certain that interest rates will continue to drop. As yields keep dropping, investors buy the long bond as it follows the other yields to lower levels.

OTHER INTEREST INFLUENCES

The Sale Of Bonds

The U.S. government borrows about $2 trillion each year by conducting some 160 auctions of Treasury securities. In addition, money is borrowed through the continuous sale of savings bonds at 40,000 locations throughout the country. Savings bonds are sold directly to individuals, whereas Treasury securities are sold to firms known as *primary dealers*, who sell to other financial institutions, who eventually sell them to individuals.

The success of Treasury auctions, determined by demand, can affect interest rates. For example, on June 8, 1998, interest rates on short-term Treasury securities rose in the Monday auction. The Treasury Department sold $5.8 billion in 3-month bills at an average discount rate of 4.995%, up from 4.945% in the previous week. The new discount rates understated the actual return to investors—5.131% for 3-month bills and 5.366% for a 6-month bill.

The Stock Market

The stock market and interest rates on debt securities are intertwined. Oftentimes, as stock prices increase, bond prices increase and interest rates decline. A look at Figure 1-6, shows clearly how interest rates and the Dow Industrials (heavy line) move in opposite directions, with high interest rates keeping stock prices down and low interest rates pushing stock prices ever higher.

FIGURE 1–6

Dow Industrials and Interest Rates 1978–1998

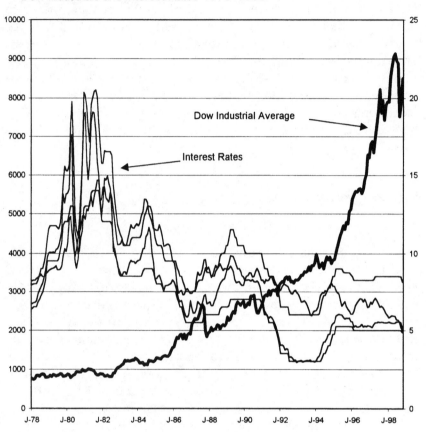

THE IMPORTANCE OF INTEREST RATES

Interest rates affect everyone, either through the rate received from investing or by causing prices to rise in times of inflation. When an investor understands the details of why and how interest rates change, that knowledge can help the investor make better selections. It's important to know that bonds purchased when interest rates were higher are worth more than face value as interest rates decline. If interest rates are low and expected to rise, there isn't much risk in investing short-term and taking advantage of the later increases.

Remember, the price of a bond is a percentage of its face value. The price is adjusted to compensate for fluctuations in the interest rates. When the bonds mature and are due for payment, the face value is repaid to the investor.

CHAPTER 2

The Coupon
Is Not Always
the Same as Yield

An investor has some bonds in an IRA account or a regular broker-age account and gets a regular statement as to the account status. The account shows the bonds with a coupon payment of 9.5%, and that's fine. However, the bonds were purchased a few years ago, and the investor has forgotten the purchase price. The investor starts to believe the bonds are earning 9.5% interest at a time when the bond yield might be 8% or less.

Understanding the difference between a bond coupon, nominal yield, and current yield is as important in bond investing as comprehending the inverse relationship of interest rates and bond prices.

COUPON

The coupon is the annualized percent of face value paid to the bondowner. The percent amount is set at the time the bond is created. Coupon is also known as the *nominal yield*. A $1000 bond with a 10% coupon (nominal yield) will make an annual payment of $100, divided into two payments of $50 every six months. Some older bonds literally have tear-off coupons to redeem for payment.

Common practice now, though, is that payments are made to the registered owner semiannually; no actual coupon is used.

CURRENT YIELD

Current yield is the coupon payment adjusted by the price paid for the bond. If an investor pays $900 for a bond that has a 10% coupon, the same two payments of $50 will be received, but the current yield, at the time of purchase, is now 11%.

Current yield = coupon dollar amount (nominal yield) ÷ price.

Strictly speaking, current yield is the nominal yield divided by the market price. If an investor owns bonds but has forgotten the yield, it can be calculated by dividing the nominal yield by the price paid by the investor. The true "current yield," based on current market price, would only be of interest to someone wanting to buy or sell.

YIELD TO MATURITY

The yield to maturity is a complicated formula that includes price, yield, and the time to maturity. The most accurate YTMs are done on a financial calculator. The purpose of YTM is to compare the overall value of one bond to another.

YIELD TO CALL

The yield to call is the same as yield to maturity except the call date is used instead of the maturity date. Call date is when the issuer is allowed to call the bonds and pay back the principal. This is often done when interest rates are dropping. The issuer calls the high interest rate and issues new bonds at lower rates, similar to individuals refinancing their home mortgages.

BUYING AT A PREMIUM

Bonds purchased for more than face value are said to be at a *premium*. Take, for example, a $1000 (face value) bond with a 6% ($60) coupon that matures in the year 2020. At maturity, the face value is returned to the bondowner. If an investor buys the bond at a price of $1200, there will be a $200 loss at maturity. The current yield on the bond is 5.0%. Why pay more than face value? Although there might be the appearance of paying something for nothing, that is not the case. The reason the bond is selling at more than face value is that interest rates have declined. The price is raised to make this bond competitive with those at the new, lower interest rate.

BUYING AT DISCOUNT

Bonds purchased for less than face value are said to be at a *discount*. Again, assume a $1000 (face value) bond with a 6% ($60) coupon that matures in the year 2020. If an investor buys the bond at $800, there are two yield considerations. First, the bond annual payment of $60 divided by the $800 price provides a current yield of 7.5%. Second, there will be a capital gain of $200 (the amount of the discount) when the bond is held to maturity at $1000.

No matter what price is paid for the bond, whether more or less, the bond will pay its face value (normally $1000) when it matures.

IMPORTANT POINT

The most important point to understand is that for any given bond, there is not always an easy number at hand that says " . . . this is my yield." Yield to the investor depends on several possibilities. The only way the investor's yield on a bond is the same as the coupon is if the bond is purchased at the face value. Keep in mind that yield is different from yield to maturity, which takes into account remaining time.

CHAPTER 3

Follow the Yield Curve

Although any bond with varying maturity lengths has a yield curve, when the term *yield curve* is discussed, it usually is in reference to United States Treasury bills, notes, and bonds. In effect, these three are all bonds, debt securities issued by the U.S. government. Bills have short maturities, notes are medium-term maturities, and the longer maturities are bonds.

WHAT IT IS

The *yield curve* is a constantly changing graph line showing interest rate levels on these Treasury securities. Figure 3–1 provides an example:

Although the main items of concern here are the 90-day T-bills and 30-year bonds, the federal discount rate and fed-funds rate are also included on this chart. On November 2, 1998, the 90-day T-bills paid interest of 4.39%, while the 30-year bonds paid 5.22%, a difference (spread) of 0.83%. The difference is not large, but this was a time when all interest rates were comparatively low. Some inversion appears in this yield curve: the 2-year has the lowest yield, the 3-year is lower than the 180-day, and the 5-year is the second-lowest yield. Also, the 20-year bond is paying more than the 30-year bond. These are considered abnormalities and could be a signal of developing economic problems.

FIGURE 3-1

Yield Curve for November 2, 1998

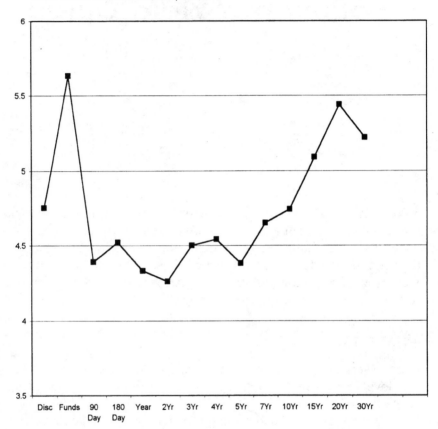

ANALYSES

Some financial analysts observe the yield-curve movements for signals of strength and weakness in the economy. Such analysis is difficult, time-consuming, and all too often arrives at incorrect conclusions. Such conclusions were possibly the source of the old joke about economists predicting nine out of the last five recessions.

NORMAL, STEEP, INVERTED, FLAT

Four descriptors often used in connection with the yield curve are normal, steep, inverted, and flat. To many, there is no such thing as

F I G U R E 3–2

Normal Yield Curve, December 1984

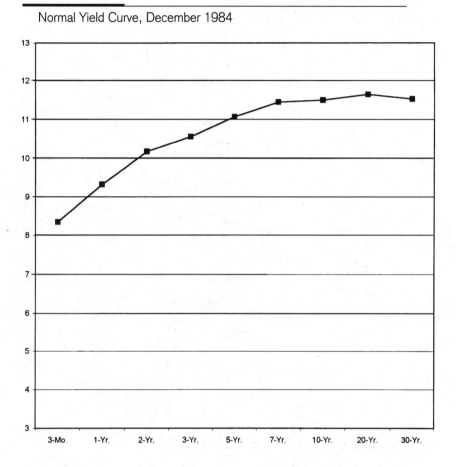

"normal" in the markets or the economy. Each day, week, month, and year has qualities that make it unique. However, the yield curve for December 1984, shown in Figure 3–2, is considered a normal yield curve.

The short-term rates are the lowest and they get higher gradually, with only a slight flattening at the end. A normal yield curve is believed to be a sign of a healthy, steady economy. The growth is slow but consistent. Stock and bond markets tend likewise to be steady. Keep in mind, though, the yield curve is not a predictor, only an indicator. Bear markets have suddenly appeared when the yield curve seemed relatively normal.

FIGURE 3–3

Normal Yield Curve, September 1994

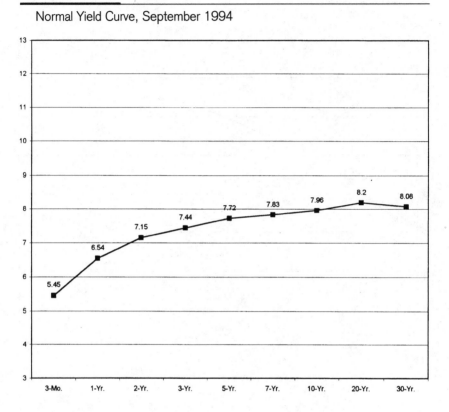

BEGINNING OF THE BIG BULL—1994

September of 1994 showed another relatively normal yield curve, with the short-term yields on the low end of the spectrum at 8.34% and the 30-year at 11.52%, a healthy 3.18% difference. As was later proven, the economy and the securities markets were stimulated to beat all previous records. See Figure 3–3.

STEEP YIELD CURVE

At times, the yield curve can be quite steep, suggesting that change could be coming to the economy. The difference between short- and long-term yields is typically about 3%, but when that increases to 4% or 5%, it creates a steeper curve (Figure 3–4). Such a curve suggests long-term bondholders believe the economy will improve

FIGURE 3–4

Steep Yield Curve, October 1992

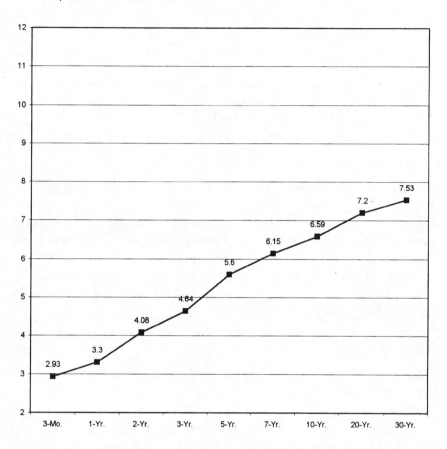

in the near future. Steep yield curves frequently appear after re-cessions as the economy stabilizes and begins expansion. Short-term investors sell out and lock in the long-term high yields, as they become available.

After the slight recession in 1991, the yield curve became steep the following April. The difference between the 3-month and the 30-year bond reached 4.12%. A year earlier, the difference between the short and long had stood at 2.38%. The gap grew until October of 1992, when it reached 4.6%. Short-term rates were forced down to make low-cost money available to stimulate business expansion. The strategy worked and business did indeed expand.

INVERTED YIELD CURVE

When short-term money pays a higher rate than long-term, it signals the opposite of expansion. This is a time of contraction. It's time to reign in the oxen and circle the wagons because the economy is overproducing and possibly heading for a recession. Interest rates are pushed up to make it more expensive to borrow money for business expansion. If action is taken soon enough, it can lessen the effects of a recession or even prevent its occurrence. (See Chapter 4, "Beware the Inverted Yield Curve.")

FLAT YIELD CURVE

On its way to inverting, the yield curve can become flattened, as shown in Figure 3–5. Although flat is considered an early warning of inversion, the curve sometimes works its way back to normal without becoming inverted. It is not unusual for a flat curve to be followed by some economic recession.

A flat yield curve will often have a slight hump in the middle area, but it is flat or nearly flat in the yield differences between the short-term and long-term Treasuries.

INDICATOR

Whereas the yield curve can be used as an indicator of possible changes in the economy as well as in the stock and bond markets, like most indicators, it is not precise. Although it can be helpful as an indicator, the yield curve should be used in conjunction with other indicators and information, including economic news and what is happening in the stock market.

INVESTMENT SELECTION

Yield-curve data can also be used directly for investment selection. If you believe interest rates are stable or likely to go lower, it might be prudent to lock in the highest yield on the 20-year bond. If you believe that interest rates are likely to rise, it might be prudent to invest in the highest short-term investment.

F I G U R E 3–5

Flat Yield Curve, October 1989

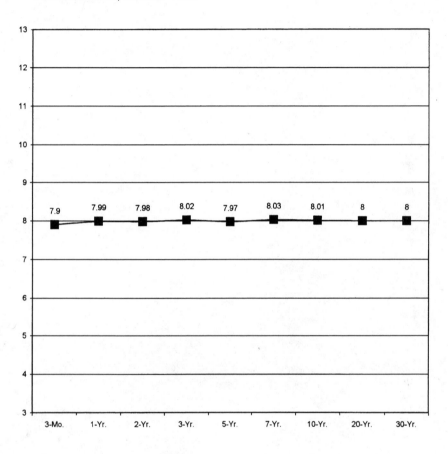

CHAPTER 4

Beware the Inverted Yield Curve

As observed in Chapter 3, the yield curve is usually upward sloping, thereby reflecting higher yields on longer-maturity bonds. Since the issuer of a bond is not obligated to repay the face value of the bond until the bond matures, the holder of the bond risks the possibility of incurring a loss. The loss can happen when the bond is sold or if the fixed-income return is less than inflation. Longer maturity dates increase the possibility of incurring a loss. Because of the higher risk, longer-maturity bonds have a higher rate of return. Also, the return is higher to persuade investors to buy the longer-term bonds.

UPSIDE DOWN

The short-term yields can actually become higher than the long-term (see Figure 4–1). The 2-year Treasury bond might pay more interest than the 20-year. Somehow that doesn't sound right. It doesn't sound fair, and it isn't. However, when short-term yields are higher, professional and individual investors are only buying the higher yields.

When the yield curve becomes inverted, it can be bearish for stocks and can become bearish for bond prices, thereby pushing interest rates temporarily higher, then ultimately lower. If interest

FIGURE 4–1

Inverted Yields, 3-Month and 30-Year Treasuries, 1977–1998

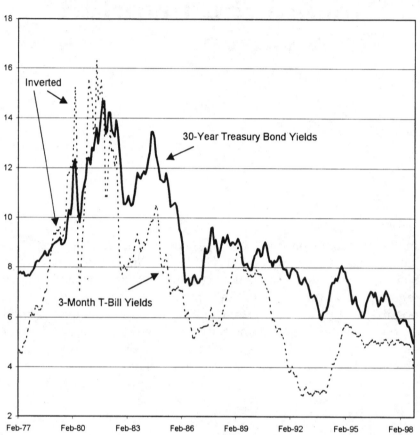

rates are already high when the yield curve inverts, steps can be taken by the Federal Reserve Board to force them down. This happened in the early 1980s.

1979 INVERSION

The yield curve inverted at the end of 1978 and remained so into 1981. Short-term yields dropped for a brief period in late summer, then took off like a rocket, moving from slightly over 9% to more than 15% by March.

FIGURE 4–2

Inverted Yield Curve, Dow Industrials, 1979–1982

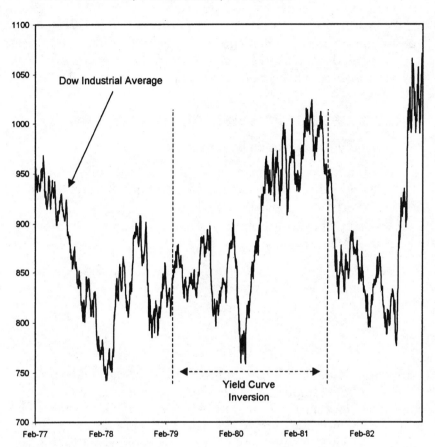

With this interest yield surge, the Dow Industrial Average plummeted more than 140 points, nearly 19%, a severe decline (Figure 4–2). The market quickly rallied back and added another 50 points and more when the yield curve settled down. In 1981, the yield curve moderated farther and the stock market improved, especially as interest rates were pushed lower.

Notice in (Figure 4–2) the volatility of the Dow Industrial Average. Some of this is due to investors' expectations of lower interest rates because of the inverted yield curve. However, the drop in interest rates took more time than expected. Buyers of stock became sellers as interest rates failed to go lower immediately. Eventually, bond yields were driven lower as investors locked in long-term high yields. In addition, the approach of the Federal Reserve was to push interest rates lower. The demand for high yields drove bond prices up, which made yields lower. The stock market reacted favorably to the lower rates as it anticipated a stronger economy ahead.

THREE CAUSES OF INVERTED YIELD CURVE

An inverted yield curve can be caused by

- An unusually high demand for short-term funds, the demand being due to some near-term liquidity problem in government or business.
- A surge in short-term inflationary pressures.
- A tightened monetary policy by the Federal Reserve.

All three—liquidity problems, inflation, and tight monetary policy—have a negative effect on the economy as well as the stock and bond markets.

INVERSION 1998

With the yield on the 30-year bond at 5.16% and the yield on the 20-year bond being higher at 5.43%, there was some inversion occurring in 1998 (Figure 4–3). However, the main concern with inversion is the short-term yield. The 90-day T-bill was at 3.95%, 1.21% less than the long bond. At this particular point in time, interest rates were considered low and the pressure to keep them low was continuing. Economic problems around the world, especially in Asia and South America, were posing some threat to the U.S. economy and creating a climate of uncertainty.

OLD BELIEF

One of the beliefs about the difference between the short- and long-term interest rates is that if the yield-curve spread is greater than 3.5%, it creates a bullish situation for the stock market. Does it? Well, yes it does, but as Figure 4–4 shows, it's not a requirement for a bull market. The chart has two lines graphed, the market as illustrated by the Standard & Poor's 500 Index and a line representing

FIGURE 4–3

Treasury Yield Curve, October 23, 1998

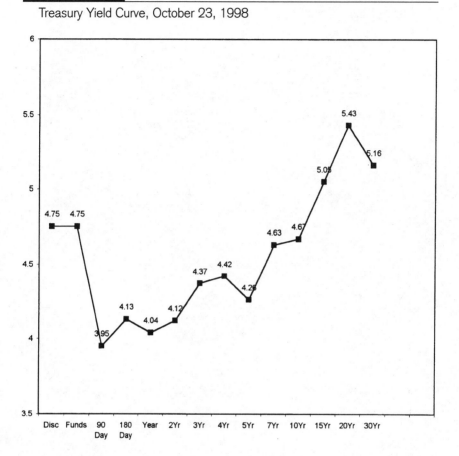

the difference in yield between the 90-day T-bills and the 30-year bond. From December of 1991 to August of 1993, the yield difference was greater than 3.5%. Another brief period during 1994 experienced a difference temporarily above that level. The stock market was nicely bullish for much of the same period. The market weakness of 1994 improved when the interest rates dropped.

LOW RATES

But look at how the stock market took off when the difference in yields dropped below the 2% level. That's where the records were broken. Does this mean the 3.5% difference concept is wrong? Not

FIGURE 4–4

Yield Spread, 3-Month and 30-Year vs. S&P 500 Index, 1990–1998

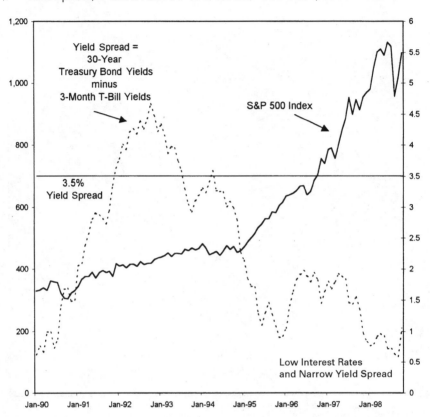

really. The example (1991–1993) did have a bullish trend. But the stock market rallied for a number of reasons, most of the credit going to low interest rates. Although the yield spread was narrowing, interest rates overall were dropping. Low interest rates stimulate the economy and businesses sell more products, thereby earning greater profits. That also tends to be the stuff of bull markets.

CHAPTER 5

There Are Four
Ways to Get a
Higher Yield on Bonds

Virtually every bond investor would like to obtain higher yields on bonds. If bonds are already owned, the investor must come up with new money or sell current bonds to buy others with higher yields. There are only a few ways to accomplish higher yields. The big four are: extend maturity; buy lower-grade, higher-risk bonds; buy short-term and reinvest as rates rise; buy long-term with a one-year noncall.

1. EXTEND MATURITY

In most situations, this is the safest way to obtain a higher bond yield. Long-term bonds tend to pay higher interest than short-term bonds. It's true of government Treasury bonds, corporate bonds, and municipal bonds. Just make certain the yield on the long bond is worth the risk of interest rate changes and the possibility of needing the money ahead of time, therefore making it necessary to sell the bond before it matures.

Although U.S. government securities are considered the safest investments in the world, active buying and selling of these securities is actually highly risky. It becomes high-risk because of the difficulty in seeing future interest rate changes. Interest rates may be

FIGURE 5–1

1-Year and 30-Year Treasury Yields, 1988–1998

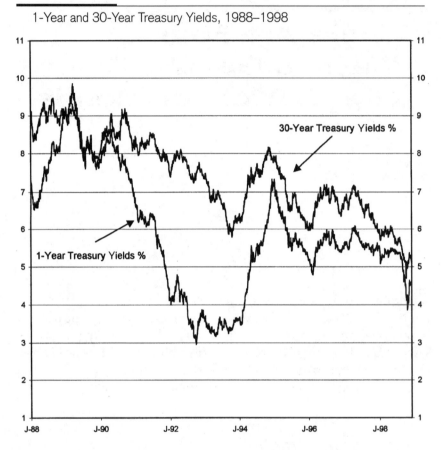

stable and secure for the present, but a year or two from now they could change dramatically. If interest rates rise, bonds bought when rates were lower will be sold at a loss.

A comparison of current yields for 1988–1998 shows how interest rates can vary in a 10-year time frame (Figure 5–1).

One of the best times to buy the 30-year bond in the past 10 years was when there wasn't much difference between the long- and short-term current yields, back in August of 1988, when yields peaked, or September 1990, while they were relatively high. However, an investor still had plenty of time to move to long-term bonds with significantly higher yields through 1991 without significant risk on bond prices. There would have been some potential erosion of bond prices in 1994, but that risk changed as interest rates came back down. If an investor had bought the long bond in October of 1993 and found it necessary to sell in November of 1994, there would have been a loss on the bond's price. Holding the bond through October of 1998 would have removed that risk for the time involved.

Difference in Yields

Observation of the difference in yields between the 1-year and the 30-year bond illustrates how dramatic the extremes can be (Figure 5–2).

FIGURE 5–2

Yield Difference (Spread) Between 30-Year and 1-Year Treasury, 1988–1998

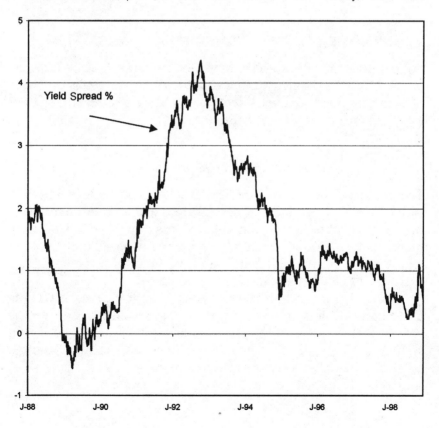

The smallest difference appeared in March of 1989, at a minus 0.4%. Yes, that's a minus, meaning the short-term 1-year bond had a higher yield than the long 30-year bond. The widest positive gap appeared in 1992, a whopping 4.33%. Over a 30-year time period, that difference can amount to serious money.

Low Interest Rates

Interest rates can only go so low. They cannot go to zero or into negative territory. If they could, the entire economic system would obviously collapse. During periods of low interest rates the decision to go to longer maturities can be a difficult one. Somewhere during such an extended time interest rates are bound to rise and have a negative impact on the long bond prices. Instead of going long, many investors will buy short-term bonds and try to do better as rates increase (see item 3 below).

2. BUY LOWER-GRADE, HIGHER-RISK BONDS

Buying investment-grade corporate bonds instead of U.S. Treasury bonds is another strategy to increase yield. The total market value of corporate bonds in the United States at the end of the first half of 1997 was an estimated $2.1 trillion.

Two Corporate Bond Markets

There are two markets for buying and selling corporate bonds. One is the New York Stock Exchange (NYSE), which trades major corporations' debt issues during the business day. There are actually more corporate bonds than stocks listed on the NYSE. That includes all nonconvertible bonds and medium-term-note issues. It excludes all U.S. federal and agency bonds.

The other market is the over-the-counter (OTC) market, made up of bond dealers and brokers around the country. They are the broker-dealer firms that trade "corporates" and other types of debt securities. The OTC market is larger than the exchange market. Most bond transactions, even those involving listed issues (also traded on the exchange), take place in this market.

F I G U R E 5–3

AAA Corporate Bonds vs. 30-Year Treasuries, 1988–1998

AAA Corporate Bonds

Although corporate bonds are higher risk than Treasuries, they are not much riskier. They receive the highest credit rating given by the bond rating services, after rigorous examination and analysis. The corporations tend to be larger, well-established, and highly profitable companies.

Three facts become obvious if you look at Figure 5–3, a chart comparing AAA corporate and 30-year Treasury bond yields.

1. Corporate yields are consistently higher.

2. The two bond yields track each other as interest rates move up or down.

3. At times, the yields are close together, and at other times they spread apart.

Another somewhat surprising fact is that the difference in yields is usually less than 1%. Figure 5–4 shows the differences in these yields, in other words, "the spread."

In the past 10 years the corporate yield advantage over the 30-year was about 0.7%. That's a difficult amount to get excited about. The low difference reinforces the idea that the AAA corporate

FIGURE 5–4

Yield Difference, AAA and 30-Year Treasury, 1988–1998

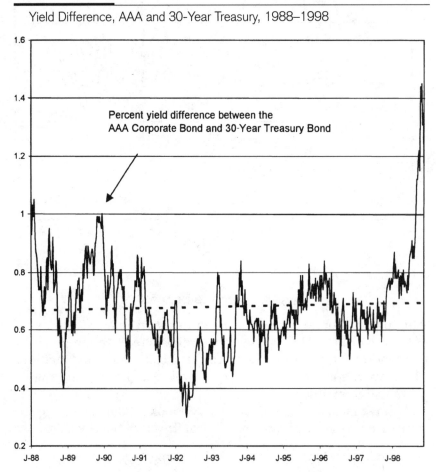

FIGURE 5–5

Yield Spread, BAA Corporate Bonds vs. 30-Year Treasury, 1988–1998

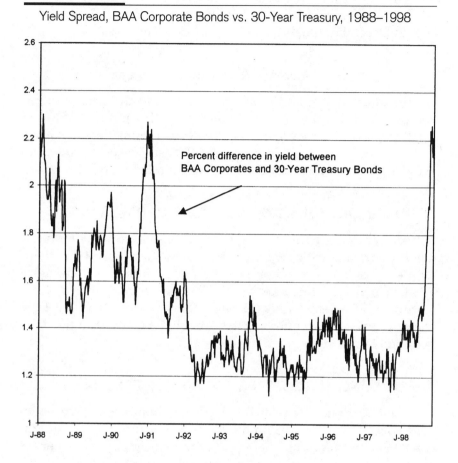

Percent difference in yield between
BAA Corporates and 30-Year Treasury Bonds

bonds aren't much riskier than the long Treasury bonds. It wasn't until 1998 that yields broke solidly through the 1% difference level, but then they only rose to 1.4%, still not much difference.

The idea of accepting higher risk for higher yields is still valid. Perhaps additional risk will do better. Look at the spread between the 30-year Treasury and a BAA corporate bond (Figure 5–5), a lower rating, but still considered good quality investment grade.

BAA Corporate Bonds

Back in December of 1990, there was a yield difference of 2.2%. Now that's looking better. Nevertheless, as interest rates dropped, the differences grew smaller. Even in 1997, the difference was only 1.14% in September, although January had a 1.41% difference, and later in December the difference was back up to 1.35%.

Don't Increase Risk with Small Steps

For the individual investor, the picture here seems clear. If one is going to increase the risk for higher yield, it cannot be done in small steps. In other words, going to the next immediate risk level, the differences are likely to be too small. Also, it seems prudent to avoid long-term investments when interest rates are relatively low.

3. BUY SHORT-TERM AND REINVEST AS RATES RISE

The idea of going with short-term bonds and eventually reinvesting in longer maturities was discussed in the first item of this chapter. Refer back to the section called Extend Maturities and Figure 5-1, which clearly illustrates the advantages to buying short-term maturities as interest rates increase. This strategy has the least amount of risk when interest rates are relatively low and have the possibility of going higher.

4. BUY LONG-TERM WITH A 1-YEAR NONCALL

When interest rates are relatively high, buy bonds that have a one-year noncall. That means no matter how low interest rates might drop, the bond cannot be called (to be refinanced) by the issuer for at least one year from issue. Noncall is also referred to as *call protection*. Obviously, it is advisable to ask about the specific call date when buying these bonds. The main added risk here is that interest rates could go higher in the one-year time frame and the bond would not be called. For most individuals that is not a serious risk, although if large amounts of principal are involved, obviously the risk increases.

Here also, this seems to be a strategy best used when interest rates are relatively high and could drop lower.

CHAPTER 6

Utility Stocks— A Higher-Yield Alternative to Bonds

Utility common stock is conservative, slow-growing, and pays quarterly dividends. Although utilities can have difficulties and go bankrupt, they really can't go out of business. That is not to say they are risk-free, but they are considered low-risk common stock. One of the great features of dividends is that they tend to increase year after year. Since the shareholder's yield is based on the original purchase price, the yield increases with the dividend.

SECOND BENEFIT

If the price of the utility common stock increases—and it usually does over time—the value of the investor's principal also increases. The combination of dividend and price increase are often referred to as *total return*, although the benefit of price increase only becomes a realized profit when the stock is sold.

THIRD BENEFIT

There is no "call" on common stock. Therefore, if interest rates decline, the investor need not be concerned that the stock will be

FIGURE 6–1

Dow Utility Average, 1988–1998

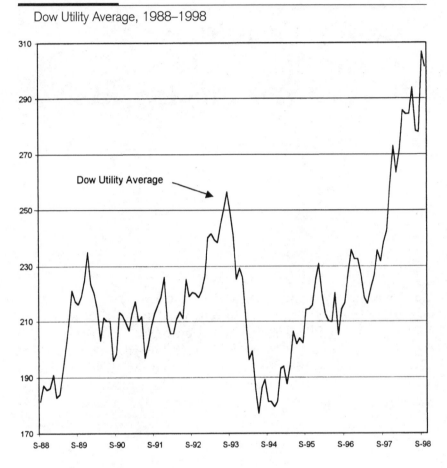

called for refinancing purposes. This also means there is no maturity date. Without a maturity date, the investor need not decide whether to go long- or short-term. The length of holding is entirely up to the investor, who can sell at any time.

DOW UTILITY AVERAGE

A look at the Dow Utility Average, a group of 15 utility stocks, shows how utility stock prices have grown in recent years (Figure 6–1). Starting in June of 1994 at a level of 177.17 points, the average grew to a peak of 306.72 points in September of 1998, a total of

129.55 points (73%). For the usually slow-growth Utility Average, that was excellent price growth.

UTILITY AVERAGE INTEREST RATE MIRROR

It has long been believed that the Dow Utility Average can act as a mirror for interest rates. As interest rates begin to rise and the yields on Treasury bonds become attractive, many investors will sell their utility stocks and buy the bonds. If the theory is true, it should mean that the Dow Utility Average would provide some early indication of approaching market weakness. However, if the Dow Industrial Average is showing strength at the same time, one can also argue that many investors are selling the slow-growth utility stocks in order to participate in strong market growth. They are buying the hot industrial, communications, or Internet stocks. It's impossible to know which factor is the dominant one. The weakening effect on the Utility Average is likely caused by a combination of the two, bond buyers wanting safer yields and stock buyers becoming more aggressive. If the threat of higher interest rates continues, all stocks and bonds can experience a selloff.

DIVIDENDS

Dividend income, that's what we are looking for, reasonably safe long-term investments that will compete with bond yields. Although it is possible to go to great depths of analysis in selecting an appropriate utility stock, here we will only look at dividends and yields.

Southern Company (NYSE: SO)

Year	1997	1996	1995	1994	1993
Dividends per share	$1.30	$1.26	$1.22	$1.18	$1.14

Southern Co. owns all the outstanding common stock of Alabama, Georgia, Gulf, Mississippi, and Savannah, each an operating public utility company. Alabama and Georgia each own 50% of the outstanding common stock of SEGCO. The operating affiliates supply electric service in the states of Alabama, Georgia,

Florida, and Mississippi, respectively, and SEGCO owns generating units at a large electric generating station that supplies power to Alabama and Georgia.

Edison International

Year	1997	1996	1995	1994	1993
Dividends per share	$1.00	$1.00	$0.75	$1.11	$1.41

Edison International is the parent corporation of Southern California Edison and four nonutility businesses: Edison Mission Energy, Edison Capital, Edison Source, and Edison EV. Southern California Edison serves 4.2 million customers. Edison Mission Energy is the owner and operator of independent power facilities. Edison Capital provides capital and financial services for energy and infrastructure projects. Edison Source provides energy and environmental services to businesses in North America. Edison EV supports the emerging electric vehicle market.

Peoples Energy (NYSE: PGL)

Year	1998	1997	1996	1995	1994	1993
Dividends per share	$1.92	$1.88	$1.84	$1.80	$1.79	$1.77

Peoples Energy Corporation is a holding company with income principally from the company's utility subsidiaries, the Peoples Gas Light and Coke Company (Peoples Gas), and North Shore Gas Company (North Shore Gas). Peoples Gas and North Shore Gas are both public utility companies, engaging in the purchase, storage, distribution, sale, and transportation of natural gas. Peoples Energy Corporation also derives income from its other subsidiaries, including Peoples Energy Resources Corp., Peoples NGV Corp., and Peoples Energy Ventures Corporation.

DIVIDENDS CAN BE CUT

The dividends of utility stock, tend to increase, but as the example of Edison International illustrates, they can experience a period of decline. Utility companies can also experience difficult economic times and might have to lower their dividend payments. Dividend payments can also be stopped. Although it is unusual for utilities to stop paying dividends, it isn't impossible.

LOOK AT THE GROWTH

The concern here is to receive a utility stock dividend that will be competitive with the yield of a 30-year Treasury bond. Take a look at Peoples Energy, where the dividends start at a level below the current treasury yield but overtake the yield in time.

Of course, this is a setup situation that has to work because we are looking back at what happened. But the point is still obvious. If a stock with a pattern of dividend growth is selected and the growth continues, it will eventually provide a yield higher than the long-term Treasury bond. In real-life investing it is also prudent to look at earnings and revenue growth, since they are the basis for increased dividends.

BUY COMMON STOCK

Let's say we purchased the common stock of Peoples Energy at a price of $20.375 back in December of 1988 (Figure 6–2). The current yield on the dividend at that time was 7.46%, with the 30-year Treasury yielding 8.95%. Once the stock or the bond is purchased, it effectively locks in the yield as long as it is owned and as long as the dividend does not change. But whereas the 30-year bond remains the same, the utility stock dividend increases each year. By 1997, the stock yield has moved above the bond yield. This is in 10 years, with 20 years remaining. By 1998, the market value (stock price) of the investment had virtually doubled. The market value of the bond had risen only a small amount, but of course, if held to maturity, it would be worth the thousand dollar original investment.

BEWARE OF EXTRA-HIGH CURRENT YIELDS

Although there are always risks when investing in common stock, a high-risk situation develops when the current yields (dividend ÷ price) appear far above the average. If a dividend yield on any common stock is 10, 20, 30, or more percentage points higher than

FIGURE 6–2

Investor View, Peoples Energy Dividend vs. the 30-Year, 1988–1998

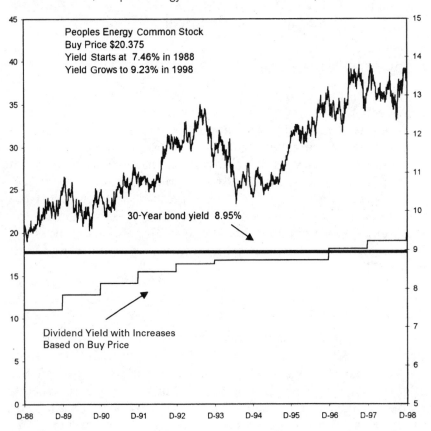

the going average, one can assume it is a high-risk situation. There is a significant probability that the dividend will be lowered or discontinued. The yield is high because investors have been selling. The selling will likely continue. The investor is often left with a stock that pays no dividend and is dropping in price.

THE INCOME STOCK

Utility common stock is also considered *income stock*. It is regularly recommended to investors looking for conservative investments that will provide a steady flow of income. Dividends are paid quarterly. It's not difficult to find utility companies that have regularly increased the annual amount of their dividends. Although the investor might have to accept a current yield lower than the current yield on bonds, the yield increases as the dividends grow. Within a few short years, the dividend yield, based on the original purchase price of the stock, can grow and surpass bond yields.

CHAPTER 7

Long Maturities Have Greater Market Risk

An investor owns a hundred 30-year bonds. The total face value is $100,000, and we'll assume the investor bought them at par (face value). The investor is suddenly hit with an expense of $20,000, and the only way to come up with the money is to sell some of the bonds.

If the current yield is the same or less than when the investor bought the bonds, there's no problem. Just sell the bonds and get the money. However, if interest rates are higher, the investor will receive less than the amount paid for the bonds. One of the added frustrations is the fact that the investor won't know the exact difference until a bid is requested for the sale of the bonds.

MARKET RISK

Market risk is the possibility of change in trading price against the investor. The investor will either lose profit or sustain a loss on the original principal invested.

LONG BOND VOLATILITY

Although long-term bond yields (with prices moving in the opposite direction) are more volatile than short-term bond yields, it's not all that simple. Because a 30-year bond exists for a long time, its yield moves around, depending on what's happening with general interest rate trends.

If interest rates are volatile, all bond yields will tend to be volatile. Obviously, the opposite is also true; if rates are stable, yields will tend to be stable.

ONE-YEAR YIELD COMPARISON

Looking at a one-year comparison of the 1-year and 30-year Treasuries shows a tendency for the yields to trend together (Figure 7–1). Notice particularly the January through April period, in which the long-bond yield is distinctly more volatile than the 1-year. The peaks are higher and the valleys are deeper. The drop from April 29 (6.03%) to November 7 (4.81%), was 1.22%, only one basis point (.01%) more than the 1-year yield decline.

FIGURE 7–1

Yield Comparison, 1-Year, 30-Year, and BAA Corporate, 12 Months, 1997–1998

It is also interesting to see that the BAA corporate bonds have somewhat less volatility than the long Treasury. As the yields drop lower on Treasuries, they remain rather firm on the higher-risk corporate.

10-YEAR YIELD COMPARISON

If the investor purchased the same hundred bonds in late 1988 and later had to sell some of them for cash, after March of 1989, there would have been some profit. Bond prices go up as yields go down. Figure 7–2 shows bond yields. Although there are many financial forces at work in this 10-year period, the Federal Reserve's

F I G U R E   7–2

Yield Comparison, 1-Year, 30-Year, and BAA Corporate, 1988–1998

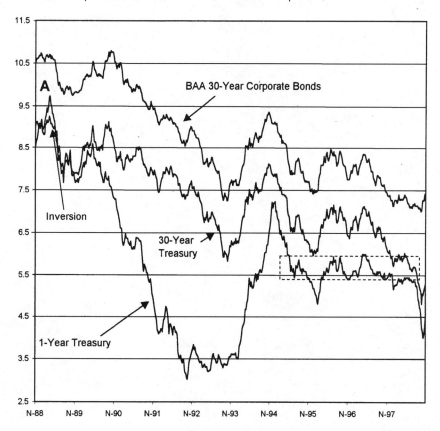

posture on lowering the interest rates was strong. Also, after the yield-curve inversion (letter A on the chart), many investors bought up long bonds believing interest rates were headed lower.

THE VOLATILITY

The difference in yield volatility remains. Notice the zigzag pattern to the 30-year yield as compared to the straighter line of the short bond. Also, as the situation begins to calm in 1995, the long bond appears more volatile. The peaks are higher and the valleys are deeper.

WHEN IS VOLATILITY A REAL PROBLEM?

The most important difficulty with volatile yields and, therefore, volatile prices is the risk that an investor might have to sell some bonds at a loss because interest rates have risen.

CHAPTER 8

Short Maturities Have Greater Reinvestment Risk

Perhaps it is a statement of the obvious, but many investors don't stop to think of this disadvantage until it's time to reinvest and they are disappointed with the lower yield.

Lower bond rates and interest rates are fuel for driving the stock market higher, but they can decrease income for the investor buying bonds. An additional headache for the short-term investor can be finding the time to reinvest. The long-term investor doesn't have to be concerned with reinvesting unless the long bonds are called or reach the maturity date. Figure 8–1 shows graphically how reinvestment can be a risk factor when investing.

Although the short-term investor enjoys all the high-interest yields, as soon as rates turn and drop, the yields decline also. In this 10-year time frame, the average short-term yield came to 7.13%. At the beginning, back in 1978, a 10-year yield of 8.03% could have been obtained.

INTEREST YIELDS DECLINING

If interest rates are declining and expected to go lower, it can be more profitable to lock in a longer rate for the higher yield. It might be on the brink of or in the early phase of a recession, when the Federal Reserve stimulates the economy with lower rates.

FIGURE 8–1

Reinvestment Risk, 3-Month vs. 10-Year Treasury, 1978–1998

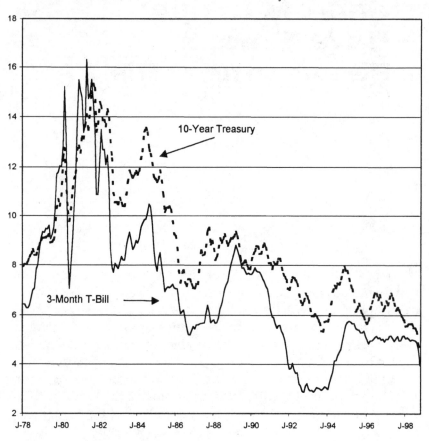

INTEREST YIELDS FLAT

If interest yields are flat, i.e., not moving up or down, obviously, the long-term will provide greater income for the investor. As shown in Figure 8–2, however, interest yields aren't often flat. They have been comparatively volatile since the late 1940s. Note how the flat period at the end of the 1990s is the longest such period since the 1940s.

Although one might be tempted to conclude that yields and interest rates usually rise after extended flat periods, such history is not always repeated. Whether or not interest rates are increased

FIGURE 8–2

Flat Yields, 3-Month T-Bills, 1934–1994

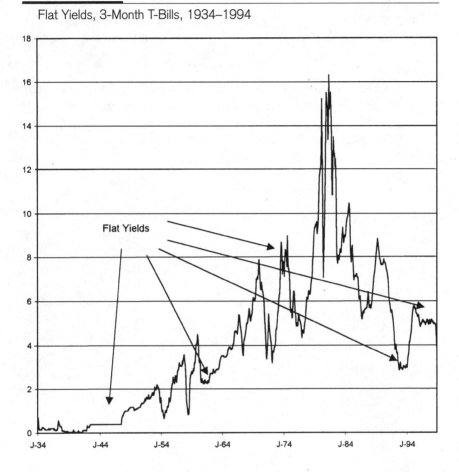

depends on economic factors more than on historic trend changes. As an example, many believed the high yields and interest rates of the late 1970s and early 1980s would continue, but such was not the case.

If yields are low and flat, they could begin to rise if the economy becomes overstimulated. However, it could take several years for interest rates to increase. Rather than having all of one's money short-term, a mixture should be considered. Referred to as "the barbell" approach, mixing involves buying both long-term and short-term bonds.

INTEREST YIELDS RISING

If interest rates and bond yields are rising, it can be time to look at short-term yields as a way to ride the trend as it moves upward. As yields peak and begin to drop, it's time to lock in some long-term money.

Buying long-term bonds as yields are increasing can mean missing an opportunity for greater income. Using short-term bonds or T-bills keeps opportunity open, with a cautionary note that the investor should avoid riding the yields up and then riding them back down again.

CHAPTER 9

Bond Funds Are Not the Same as Bonds

There can be significant differences between owning bonds and bond funds. Bond funds can be appealing because of diversification safety and selection by professional managers. Funds are often good at allaying investors' fears about selecting individual bonds, but investors need to be wary and careful with their fund selections. Some have higher risk than others.

BOND FUNDS NOT FIXED INCOME

Bond funds can be more complicated than bonds themselves because contrary to what the name implies, they are not really fixed-income investments. Even when a bond mutual fund's portfolio is made up entirely of bonds, the fund itself has neither a fixed yield nor a contractual obligation to return principal at a maturity date, two major characteristics of individual bonds.

CHANGING RISK

In addition, bond fund managers trade their positions. Therefore, the risk-return profile of a bond mutual fund is always changing. The risk level of an actual bond declines the longer it is held by an investor. Risk goes lower with every interest payment. A bond mutual fund can increase or decrease in risk at the whim of the manager.

In any bond mutual fund, the manager might also be given flexibility to increase the yield with securities other than bonds. The 1990s saw some funds losing hundreds of millions of dollars trying to increase fund yields with derivatives. If the manager's guess is incorrect, it can be devastating for the fundholders.

TWO BASIC TYPES OF BOND FUNDS

Although new investment products are being created every year, there are essentially two types of bond funds.

Open-End Fund

One is called an *open-end mutual fund*. It is run by a portfolio manager who decides when and how to make changes by buying and selling bonds in the fund. This type of fund carries risk. It is a true mutual fund, diversified into several bond issues. The reason it has risk is that there is no way a shareholder can hold a bond to maturity. Maturity has effectively been removed as a variable. If bonds in the fund do reach maturity, they are replaced and the fund continues, without returning the principal to the investor. An investor has to redeem shares to get the money back, and that's the same as selling.

The fund has money continually coming in as well as money going out to pay holders who have redeemed their shares. Shares can be redeemed at any time the investor chooses. The flexibility given to the fund manager to increase yield is risk in this type of fund.

Closed-End Fund

A closed-end fund (unit trust) acts much like a bond. It does have a maturity date. It has a set number of shares to be purchased by investors. When the bonds mature, the principal is returned to share-owners. The only way to buy shares of a closed-end fund is either to buy them new (when issued) or buy shares someone else is selling (in the secondary market). Although this has some effect on liquidity, it is still relatively easy to buy or sell shares of a closed-end bond fund.

THE DIFFERENCE IS MATURITY

One of the most important safety features of a bond is that it can be held to maturity, and the investor can receive the return of the bond's face value. If that feature is removed, the investment becomes high-risk. Prices and yields of bond funds fluctuate on a daily basis. The yield is not "locked in" at a specific percentage as it would be with the actual bonds. If interest rates rise, the share values of the bond funds are lowered. The impact is nearly immediate. If the owner of actual bonds encounters a rise in interest rates, the owner can avoid taking the loss by holding the bonds to maturity.

RISK RATINGS FOR BOND FUNDS

Risk ratings for bond mutual funds have become of interest lately. The National Association of Securities Dealers (NASD) and The Investment Company Institute have fought to keep funds from referring to their bond fund rating in their sales literature. The fear is that investors will misunderstand or misinterpret the meaning of the ratings. Because individual bond ratings mostly have a reliable reputation, it is feared the confidence will be unduly transferred to bond fund ratings, which are not as uniform and don't have much of a track record.

KNOW WHAT TYPE OF FUND

Does that mean investors should avoid bond funds? Not necessarily. Bond funds can be suitable for investors who know why they are going into these funds and what they expect in return.

Many funds require initial investments of $3000 or less, with the ability to add smaller amounts on a monthly basis. Oftentimes, the money can be transferred directly from a bank account to the fund. Mutual funds have programs for withdrawing money on a regular basis, which is more convenient than selling bonds to raise cash. Many funds pay interest on a monthly basis rather than every six months.

WEIGH THE RISKS AND BENEFITS

When considering a bond mutual fund, become aware of the risks involved. Even if a fund invests in "government securities," it doesn't mean the fund is less exposed to risk. In fact, such funds often are hit the hardest by an increase in interest rates.

Weighing the advantages and risks can help an individual decide whether to invest in bond mutual funds, bond unit trusts, or actual bonds.

Buy Bonds That Won't Outlive You

"I buy bonds that won't outlive me." Brokers hear this or similar statements nearly every day. They call a fixed-income client to tout a 20- or 30-year bond with good safety and a respectable yield. The client listens patiently until the maturity date is mentioned. "I'm not going to live that long," the investor says, and it's a serious objection. Although the broker may be tempted to ask if the client intends to spend all the money before dying, it would be rude to do so. Most often, a shorter-term, lower-yielding bond is selected.

WHY THE CONCERN

So why do some people think they have to outlive their fixed-income investments? Is it a real objection, or does it hide other concerns? Does it give them a feeling of being in control, or is it just a feeling of keeping things orderly? Stock investors don't seem to mind the fact that common stock never reaches a maturity date, so why should bond investors be concerned?

PRINCIPAL RETURNED AT MATURITY

Perhaps the difference lies in the concept of having the principal, or face value, of the bond returned when it reaches the maturity date.

People can easily accept getting money back from stock only by selling and taking a profit. With a bond, however, the investor puts up the money, but the principal is returned at the end of a specific time period. It's a different way of looking at investing. Stocks can be sold at any time, but many bond investors think in terms of buying a bond and holding it until maturity.

BUY AND SELL BONDS

The fact that bonds can be bought and sold in a manner similar to stocks is seldom even considered by these investors. Although buying and selling long-term bonds adds an element of risk to price changes if interest rates change, it can be done. The investor can get some idea of any potential gain or loss on bond price changes by watching the brokerage monthly statement. Price changes are noted if the bonds are held in the brokerage account. Also, an investor can request a firm bid from a broker, although the firm might require the bonds to be deposited in order to obtain a price quotation.

Consider, too, that even short-term bonds might outlive the investor. Life is filled with unexpected events, some of them tragic. When the bonds outlive the investor, they simply become part of the estate like other investments and properties.

CONSIDER FACTORS OTHER THAN LONGEVITY

The maturity of investment bonds can be important in some situations. If the investor expects to need the principal invested in the next few years, it can be prudent to take the lower yield on the 2-year bond rather than risk price changes with the longer maturity.

If an investor believes that interest rates will rise significantly in the next few years, it might be a good strategy to stay with the shorter maturities. Even if the bonds have to be sold, short-term bond prices fluctuate less than long-term bond prices. The shorter maturity could be the better strategy.

CHAPTER 11

Invest in Bonds If You Want Steady, Fixed Returns

Steady, fixed returns are what bonds were originally designed to provide. Remember, a bond is a loan of money to a company, government, or other organization. Interest normally is paid every six months until the maturity date or call date is reached. If the bond is called or the maturity date is reached, the face value of the bond is returned to the investor.

BOND CALLS

A *call* is a feature on a bond that allows the issuer to cash in the bond early. Calls are often stipulated as one-year calls or five-year calls. The purpose of the call is to provide a benefit to the issuer. If interest rates are declining, bond issuers don't want to be paying 10% or more when rates have fallen to 8%. They call the high-rate bonds and issue new bonds at the current interest rates.

On the other hand, investors won't be interested in buying bonds that might be called shortly thereafter. Call protection is an added feature that says the bonds cannot be called for a certain amount of time. The bonds cannot be called until the call date is reached. If interest rates have dropped low enough by the call date, the bond is called.

A call and issue of new bonds might be compared to a home-owner refinancing a mortgage. Homeowners can refinance at any time, although they are not likely to do so unless interest rates have dropped low enough. A new mortgage is obtained and the old, higher-interest mortgage is paid up.

Corporate bond issues commonly have a call provision. U.S. Treasuries have in the past had call provisions. The last time they existed was back in the early 1980s when interest rates were un-usually high.

1988

Go back to the year 1988, in March. The stock market was still act-ing cautious after a record 508-point, one-day drop in the Dow Industrial Average. In effect, that was a bear market in one trading session of the stock market. There had been pressure from the Federal Reserve to move interest rates lower, although there was an upward surge following the market correction.

INTEREST-RATE TREND

It's the first of March, and an investor graphs interest-rate yields on the 1-year and 30-year Treasuries, the data being obtained from the Federal Reserve Bank of Chicago.[1] Ten years are graphed to get a feel for the long-term trend (Figure 11–1).

Seeing the downward interest rate trend and knowing the Federal Reserve intended to continue the pressure unless it became inflationary, an investor could easily have decided to buy some long-term bonds.

YIELD CURVE OF 1988

On March 2, 1988, the investor decides to look at the yield curve to see how much yield advantage exists in the spread between Treasuries and corporates. Sometimes the spread is so small there's not enough advantage for the added risk.

The yield curve (Figure 11–2) shows the AAA corporate bonds are yielding 9.27%, BAA bonds 10.48%, and the A-UTIL 9.78%.

---

1 In 1998, the investor can download this data from the Internet.

F I G U R E 11–1

Yield Trend, Treasury Bonds, 1978–1988

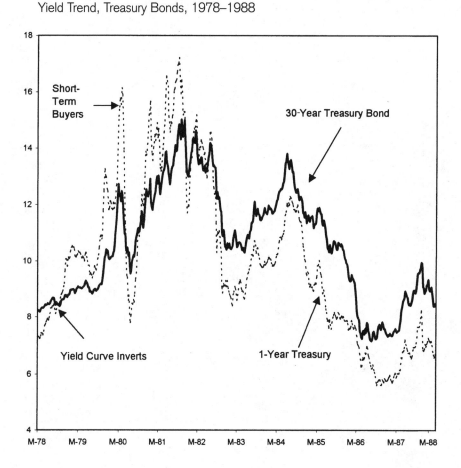

With the 30-year Treasury bond at a yield of 8.41%, the investor decides to go with the 30-year, 5-year no call (the bonds cannot be called for five years) corporate bonds.

$30,000 TO INVEST

Another investor decides to invest equal amounts of $10,000 into three separate risk categories: AAA, BAA, and A-UTIL (A-rated utility bonds).

F I G U R E 11–2

Yield Curve and Corporate Yields, March 2, 1988

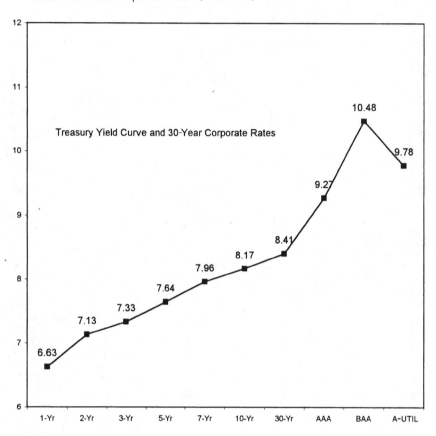

The investor buys:

Quantity	Rating	Maturity and Type	Current Yield
10	AAA	30-year (5-year no call) corporate bonds	9.27%
10	BAA	30-year (5-year no call) corporate bonds	10.48%
10	A	30-year (5-year no call) utility bonds	9.78%

With these bonds, the investor earns $1,476.50 every six months for an annual total of $2953. The combined yield of the

Buy Bonds, March 2, 1988

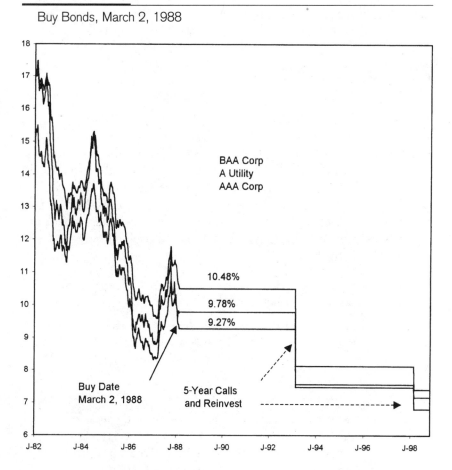

three bonds is an annual 9.8%. These amounts are locked in for at least five years, at which point the bonds will likely be called. If interest rates remain unchanged or rise, the bonds probably won't be called. At the time of this bond purchase, it was quite likely the bonds would be called. (See Figure 11–3).

BONDS ARE CALLED

We fast-forward to March 1993, when the bonds are called, the $30,000 in principal is returned, and the investor must buy new bonds. For the purposes of this example, the same three types of corporate bonds will be selected, although they might not be the best selections. Alternative strategies will also be examined.

MARCH 3, 1993, YIELD CURVE

What does the yield curve show? For March 3, 1993, the yield curve was basically normal, with the short 1-year at 3.31% and the long 30-year at 6.85% (Figure 11–4). The spread to corporates was reasonable: the AAA at 7.56%, the BAA at 8.12%, but the A Utility was at a disappointing 7.47%. Since the moderately higher-risk utility bond had a lower yield than the AAA corporate, it would obviously make more sense to double up on the safer bond. But for purposes of this example, the investor stays with the diversification of the three bonds and again invests $10,000 in each category.

The investor buys:

Quantity	Rating	Maturity and Type	Current Yield
10	AAA	30-year (5-year no call) corporate bonds	7.56%
10	BAA	30-year (5-year no call) corporate bonds	8.12%
10	A	30-year (5-year no call) utility bonds	7.47%

Now the investor earns an annual $2315, a more modest 7.7% overall annual yield on the three types of bonds. It means $638 a year less. For someone on a fixed income, that can be a significant reduction of earnings. However, the income is locked in, at least for the next five years. A check of the interest rate trend shows that rates are still dropping lower in 1993 (Figure 11–5).

THE 1993 BONDS ARE CALLED

It wasn't unexpected. The trend was down. The attitude of the Federal Reserve was to keep interest rates down. Therefore, the five-year calls were activated. The $30,000 principal is returned to the investor. It's time to look at the bond yields again.

FIGURE 11–4

Yield Curve and Corporate Yields, March 3, 1993

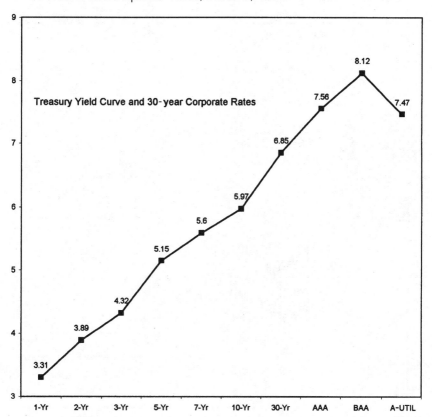

1998 YIELD CURVE

Notice how flat the March 4, 1998, yield curve has become (Figure 11–6). Yield curves often go flat before inverting. In fact, there is a small inversion between the 7-year and 10-year bonds. The curve suggests that interest rates could go even lower.

Also, notice the 0.81% spread between the 30-Year treasury Bond and the AAA corporate. Although it looks greater than the others do, it isn't. The yield curve of 1988 and 1993 both had spreads of 0.86% between the AAA corporate and Treasury bonds.

FIGURE 11–5

Buy Bonds, March 3, 1993

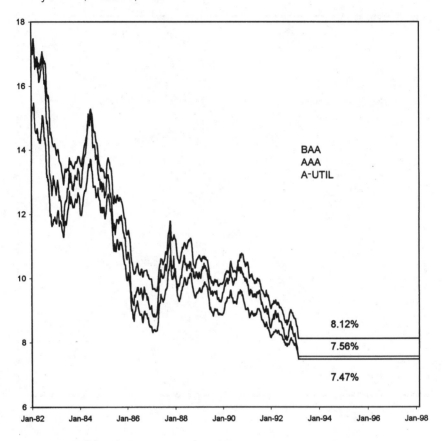

REINVEST LONG-TERM

Although many investors would be tempted to stay short-term with the low yields of March 1998, for this example, the investor again buys the 30-year bonds.

The investor buys:

Quantity	Rating	Maturity and Type	Current Yield
10	AAA	30-year (5-year no call) corporate bonds	6.81%
10	BAA	30-year (5-year no call) corporate bonds	7.71%
10	A	30-year (5-year no call) utility bonds	7.40%

FIGURE 11-6

Yield Curve and Corporate Yields, March 4, 1998

The investor now earns $2192 annually for a combined yield of 7.31%, with bonds less likely to be called.

STEADY, FIXED RETURNS

Although bonds do provide a "steady, fixed return," the example given here shows how much that concept depends on interest rate movements. Obviously, locking in long-term yields is a good strategy when rates are high and beginning to drop. A shorter-term or other strategy can be better when yields are low.

Invest in Bonds If Your Risk Profile Is Lower

What's a risk profile? It's a series of questions to determine the investment risk a person is willing to accept. Most such profiles are usually brief and quickly narrow the analysis to a specific type of bond, stock, or mutual fund. Although they do some assessment of risk tolerance, in most situations the purpose of such a profile is to sell investments. In other words, the purpose is to convince the investor that the recommended investment fits into the profile. This is not to criticize or condemn the use of such profiles, but to urge some caution regarding the conclusions drawn from the answers given.

ALL INVESTMENTS HAVE RISK

When many would-be investors are asked how much risk they can accept, their answer is, None. "In fact, there are no investments without risk. That includes Treasury bonds, certificates of deposit, savings and checking accounts, even cash. Cash earns no interest, so it has inflation risk. Savings and checking accounts pay low interest and have inflation risk. Certificates of deposit (CDs) have lower yields and reinvestment risk. Since it's impossible to invest with no risk, it becomes necessary to estimate an amount of acceptable risk.

PROFILE CRITERIA

The following list gives examples of the types of information covered in many investor risk profiles.

1. Time Frame and Age

The time frame might be geared to things like buying a house, saving for the children's college education, or retirement. Longer time frames can afford to take more risk. The belief here is that if a mistake is made on a bad investment, there is enough time to correct the problem with a good investment.

The same reasoning holds for age. If an investor is at or nearing retirement and has limited financial assets, it is prudent to moderate risk. However, larger net worth individuals can still afford to have some of their assets in riskier investments.

2. What Is the Investment Objective

Objectives are often talked about, but action is seldom taken to clarify definitions or to implement the objectives. Brokerage firms are required to know an individual's investment objectives and will often use four categories to determine which types of securities to recommend. They are:

Income
Growth
Total return
Speculation

These categories relate directly to the type of investments to be used to reach a specific financial goal. Although most individual bond investors are looking for current income, when a significant decline in yields pushes up bond prices, the total return can begin to look attractive. The only disadvantage is the need to sell the bonds to take advantage of the price increases.

Objectives can also be defined in terms of intended use of the money, such things as:

- Education
- A home
- A second home or lake cabin

- Retirement income
- Buying a business

It doesn't matter what objective an investor chooses, when it is specifically defined and clearly stated, the probability of success is greatly increased.

3. Willingness to Accept Loss

Here is the meat and potatoes of a risk profile. The ability to truly accept the risk of investment loss gets to the nitty-gritty of what the profile is all about. Although many beginning investors balk at admitting such willingness, they probably have similar risks in their current investments. The risk is often not realized or understood, but it does exist. Investing has risk just as life has risk. Rather than a futile attempt to avoid risk, it's better to develop an understanding and moderate it wherever possible.

4. Market Knowledge

Although an investor's market knowledge can be an important aspect of a risk portfolio, it also helps the sales representative decide how much time to spend with a customer. Brokers and other securities sales representatives will often go to great lengths to educate their customers whenever they can. However, the salesperson's job is not to educate; rather, it is to sell securities. A prospect with good market knowledge will probably receive more attention than a beginner.

5. Understanding of Risk-Reward

The paradox of risk-reward in investing is simple: Although higher-reward investments usually contain higher risk, higher-risk investing does not necessarily mean higher rewards. The key word here is *risk*. When misunderstood, it can lead to disaster.

Look at the basic idea: "If I take greater risk, I'll get greater rewards." With this in mind, an investor buys $100,000 worth of junk bonds for fifty cents on the dollar. No other analysis is performed. The bonds default; the company goes out of business and liquidates. Most likely, the investor can kiss the money goodbye. After the legal fees and creditors are paid, there probably won't be any money left to pay the bondholders.

Beginning investors should be willing to accept risk for reward, but they should also understand how much risk is involved. Learn the difference between a AAA-rated and a B-rated bond. Avoid nonrated (junk) bonds until some understanding develops. Start conservatively and gradually or partially begin to accept more risk.

6. Other Investment, Savings, or Retirement Programs

Those who have additional investment programs automatically have less risk. If a new investment program has trouble or fails, the others provide diversification so the investor doesn't lose everything.

WHY BROKERS DON'T DISCUSS RISK

If securities sales representatives spent too much time defining and describing the investment risk in bonds, no one would buy any. Brokers and other sales reps need to sell securities to earn an income. In many situations, they will give details when asked, but they will have a tendency to downplay risk.

COMPLETE THE PROFILE

As an investor, you should complete a risk profile for the investments, decide if the results are in a reasonable comfort range, and proceed with the investing. If the profile seems too risky, move a notch toward conservatism. It probably won't make any difference to a sales representative. They usually aren't paid more for selling higher-risk investments.

CHAPTER 13

Invest in Bonds If You Do Not Want Capital Erosion

If an investor buys a bond and holds the bond until it matures, the face value of the bond is returned. Because this is true (assuming there are no defaults), bonds do not experience *capital erosion*. This can be compared to a dividend-paying stock held for a similar time period and sold. If the stock price were higher at selling time, there would be a profit. If the stock price were lower, there would be a loss, or erosion, of capital.

However, this is too simplistic. It is possible to have capital erosion with bonds if the total picture of principal and income is considered. This is a discussion of actual bonds and not bond mutual funds.

MUTUAL FUNDS ARE DIFFERENT

Open-end bond mutual funds don't have a maturity date for the investor. Money is constantly flowing in and out of the fund. As bonds mature, they are replaced with new bonds. The fund shares are priced according to the value of the underlying securities. If interest rates trend upwards, the value of bond mutual fund shares will drop. If the investor needs to sell, it might be at a loss. Closed-end bond funds do have a maturity date and therefore act more like individual bonds. They can be held to maturity.

SOURCES OF CAPITAL EROSION

There are three primary sources of capital erosion:

- Inflation
- Price Impact
- Opportunity Loss

Inflation with CPI and PPI

Inflation can comprise several factors, but it is basically the increase of wages and prices in an economic system. A small amount of inflation is positive because it shows a healthy, growing economy. The Consumer Price Index and the Producer Price Index are often looked at for inflationary trends. In the U.S., these indexes are reported by the Division of Information Services of the Bureau of Labor Statistics. Contact for information can be made in the following ways:

- Website: http://stats.bls.gov/blshome.html
- Email: blsdata@bls.gov
- Telephone: Information hours are 8:30 a.m. to 4:30 p.m., Eastern Time
  Phone: (202) 606-5886
  Fax: (202) 606-7890
  Recording: (202) 606-7828
- Address:
  Division of Information Services
  2 Massachusetts Avenue, NE Room 2860
  Washington, D.C. 20212
- TDD: To use the TDD system for the hearing impaired: (202) 606-5897.

What Is the Consumer Price Index

According to the U.S. Bureau of Labor Statistics, the Consumer Price Index (CPI) is a measure of the average change over time in the prices paid by consumers for a fixed market basket of consumer goods and services. The CPI provides a way to compare what a basket of goods and services costs this month with what it cost a month or a year ago.

What Is the Producer Price Index?

Again, according to the U.S. Bureau of Labor Statistics, the Producer Price Index (PPI) is a family of indexes that measures the average change over time in the selling prices received by domestic producers of goods and services. The PPI measures price change from the viewpoint of the seller, the Consumer Price Index from the viewpoint of the consumer. Sellers' and purchasers' prices may change differently owing to such things as government subsidies, sales and excise taxes, and distribution costs.

Figure 13–1 shows a steady upward slant with some tapering in 1997. Notice the bump in 1990 and the steeper line back in the

F I G U R E 13–1

Inflation, CPI, and PPI, 1968–1998

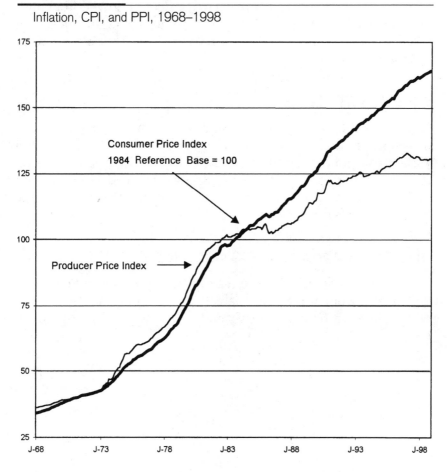

late 1970s. "Runaway inflation" and "inflationary spiral" were among the expressions being used to describe inflation in the late 1970s and early 1980s.

The Main Point

Inflation does cause capital erosion in bond investing. However, it causes similar capital erosion with most other investments unless they increase in value because of inflation—e.g., real estate, collectibles, and so forth.

PRICE IMPACT

Increases in inflation normally lead to higher interest rates and bond yields. As bond yields rise, bond prices go lower. If a bond-holder needs to sell before the maturity date, it could mean selling at less than face value and a loss for the investor. This is also a form of capital erosion.

OPPORTUNITY LOSS

Opportunity loss is not really capital erosion, but it does mean missing out on higher income. If an investor buys bonds with a yield of 6% and bond yields increase to 8%, the investor is missing out on the higher income. Selling the lower yield bonds would mean selling at a loss. There probably wouldn't be any advantage to selling and buying the higher yields.

DON'T LET CAPITAL EROSION GET IN THE WAY

The fact that bonds can have some capital erosion should not deter the investor from purchasing them. It is more important to focus on where interest rates are currently and where they might be going in the near future.

CHAPTER 14

Why T-Bills
Can Be Risky

What is a Treasury bill (commonly called a T-bill)? It is a discount debt security (meaning no coupon, it's bought at less than face value), issued by the U.S. government for periods of less than one year. T-bills are issued in 3-month, 6-month, and 12-month maturities; in minimum denominations of $1,000; with multiples of $1,000 thereafter. Individuals can buy T-bills directly from the Federal Reserve's weekly auctions or in the secondary market for virtually any desired maturity. Secondary market T-bills can be purchased from or sold to banks or brokerage firms for a small fee.

BEST RATING

Although there is never an official rating given to direct U.S. government debt securities, they are considered to be the safest in the world. If there were such a rating as AAA+, it would be given to U.S. Treasury bills, bonds, and notes. T-bills are considered risk-free investments. They are even safer than insured certificates of deposit that are backed by the F.D.I.C. They are considered safer because they are a direct obligation of the U.S. government rather than being guaranteed by a government agency. Interest rate risk is minimal due to the short-term nature of T-bills, but as Figure 14–1 illustrates, the difference between long- and short-term can be significant.

20-YEAR COMPARISON

If an investor back in October of 1978 believed interest rates had peaked and the investor bought a 30-year Treasury bond, the buy would have locked in a rate of 8.08%. On a $10,000 investment, the investor would receive $808 a year for the next 30 years, or until the year 2008. Obviously, the long-term investor would have been unhappy during the early years, since the 30-year rate rose as high as 15.69% in July of 1981. That would have been an additional $771 a year for at least five years (when rates were high, the long bonds had a five-year call option).

By the end of 1988, the long-term investor had total interest of $8080, while the short-term investor did better at $9875. At the beginning of 1989, the short-term investor would have done well to lock in a long-term rate. Interest rates were effectively being forced lower and the pressure continued. In 1998, at the end of 20 years, the long-bondholder had earned interest of $16,160, and the income had been steady and predictable. The short-term buyer of 90-day T-bills had earned interest of $15,170. A difference of $990 over a period of 20 years is not a lot of money. However, many individuals who buy Treasury securities are investing hundreds of thousands of dollars. Some are investing millions. The difference can quickly become significant.

REINVESTMENT RISK

The main risk of continual short-term investing is reinvesting at lower interest rates. Although the T-bills will follow interest rates up and down, during periods of change like the 1980s, it can be more profitable to lock in something long-term. The example shown in Figure 14–1 is only a modest (8.08%) long-term rate. Obviously, the difference between the long-bond yield and three-month T-bills would be greater if a higher rate had been selected. The long bond hit a top at 15.69% in July of 1981, and then rates headed lower. It wasn't until April of 1993 that the long bond hit bottom at 4.43%.

THE POINT IS

Interest rates usually change slowly over a period of several months or years. A short-term-bond investing strategy can be pru-

FIGURE 14–1

20-Year Yield Comparison, T-Bills vs. 30-Year Treasury Bond, 1978–1998

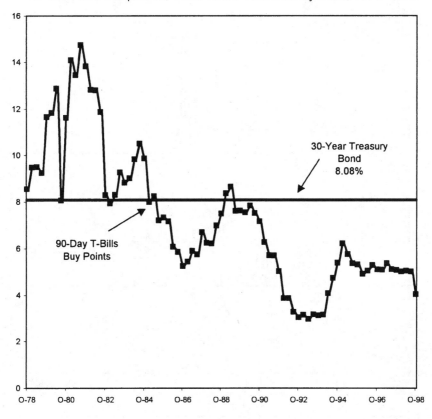

dent when interest rates are low and likely to go higher. A long-term strategy will tend to be more profitable when interest rates are higher. Figure 14–2 shows the 3-month T-bill yields for the past 40 years.

It is obvious that the December 1998 rates are comparatively low. They might go higher, they can go lower, or they can remain flat. Any changes will be due to economic conditions and the actions taken by the Federal Reserve Bank.

F I G U R E 14–2

Interest Rates, 3-Month T-Bills, 1958–1998

CHAPTER 15

Know the Bond Options

Bond options can be traded by individuals where appropriate and suitable. However, bond options are largely a product for institutional trading. For example, some of the largest covered call option sellers are government bond funds. They sell covered calls to enhance their portfolio yields. The use of covered calls, where calls are sold on securities owned, is a conservative strategy. The information presented here is a brief explanation of how bond options function.

WHAT IS AN OPTION

An *option* is the right, but not the obligation, to buy or sell a security for a specified price (*strike price*) on or before a specific date (*expiration date*). A *call* is the right to buy a security, and a *put* is the right to sell a security. The investor who purchases an option, whether it is a put or a call, is the option "buyer." Conversely, the one who originally sells the put or call is the option "seller." The specified price is called the strike price, often simply referred to as "strike."

When a bond option is "exercised," the bonds are called by the bond buyer and put to the put seller at the strike price. Only the option holder (buyer) is allowed to exercise the terms of an option. American-style options can be exercised at any time. European-style options can only be exercised on the specified expiration date. Most options are American-style.

CAUTION

Options can be high risk. Before trading options, a person should take the time to learn about them in detail. All new options traders should obtain copies of *Characteristics and Risks of Standardized Options*.

Copies of this document are available from your broker or from the:

Chicago Board Options Exchange
400 S. LaSalle Street
Chicago, IL 60605

The OCC Prospectus contains information on options issued by The Options Clearing Corporation. Copies of this document are available from:

The Options Clearing Corporation
440 S. LaSalle Street, 24th Floor
Chicago, IL 60605

PRICES

An option's price consists of the option's intrinsic value and time value. Intrinsic value ("in-the-moneyness") is the value of the option if it were immediately exercised.

Call's Intrinsic Value

The intrinsic value of a call whose strike price is less than the market price is equal to the market price of the underlier less the strike price. The intrinsic value of a call whose strike price is greater than the market price of the underlier is zero.

Strike Price Less

When the strike price of a call is less than the underlying security's market price:

Intrinsic value = market price of
the underlying security − strike price of the option

Example:

Bond at a price of 100 (= $1000)
Call strike price 97 (= $970)
Intrinsic value = 3 (= $300)

Strike Price Greater

When the strike price of a call is more than the underlying security's market price:

$$\text{Intrinsic Value} = \text{zero}$$

Put's Intrinsic Value

The intrinsic value of a put whose strike price is greater than the market price of the underlier is equal to the strike price less the market price. The intrinsic value of a put whose strike price is less than the market price of the underlier is zero.

Strike Price Greater

When the strike price of a put is greater than the underlying security's market price:

$$\text{Intrinsic Value} = \text{strike price of the option} - \\ \text{market price of the underlying security}$$

Strike Price Less

When the strike price of a put is less than the underlying security's market price:

$$\text{Intrinsic value} = \text{zero}$$

Example:

Bond at a price of 100 (= $1000)
Put strike price 97 (= $970)
Intrinsic value = 0 (= $0)

At-, Out of-, and In-the-Money

Options can be written (sold) at-the-money, where the strike price is equal to the market price of the underlying security. They can be written out-of-the-money, where there would be a negative value if the option were immediately exercised. Or they can be written in-the-money, where there would be a positive value if the option were exercised immediately. Only in-the-money options have intrinsic value. The three perspectives are always as viewed from the option holder's (buyer's) viewpoint.

TIME VALUE

Time value is essentially the potential future value of the option. Time value decreases as an option moves closer to the expiration date.

PROFITS

The seller (*writer*) of an option receives the premium (*selling to open a position*) and profits if the option premium drops lower, where it can be repurchased (*buying to close a position*), or the option can be allowed to expire worthless. The buyer (*holder*) profits if the premium rises, where the option can be sold at a profit or can be exercised.

OTC

Many large primary dealers and a few large active dealers make markets in over-the-counter (OTC) Treasury bond options. Other firms might use Treasury bond options in their own proprietary trading or investing accounts.

> Dealers prefer to trade options on Treasuries that have on-the-run[1] issues as underliers because, as speculators, they prefer to trade the most liquid issues. Customers more often trade options on Treasuries that use off-the-run[2] issues as underliers because, as investors, they prefer to trade options written on issues they already own.[3]

---

1 The most recently issued bonds in each maturity.

2 Bond issues auctioned previous to the most recent auction.

3 Christina I. Ray, *The Bond Market, Trading and Risk Management*, McGraw-Hill, New York, 1993.

FLEXIBILITY

OTC options on Treasury bonds are able to have any underlying Treasury issue, strike price, or expiration date. These details are limited only by dealers' imaginations and market viewpoint. They can expire any time from 4:00 p.m. (Eastern Standard Time) on the same day the option is written to three months later. Apparently, most options are written with a month or less to expiration. Obviously, the flexibility can be good for what a trader wants to do, but it can affect the trading liquidity of some options.

MOSTLY INSTITUTIONAL

Although bond options trading is largely the realm of institutional investors, who have hundreds of millions of dollars to work with, individual investors should be aware of their existence and might be able to use them in the right situation. Also, things change. Bond options could become more popular with individuals and become another product for hedging or speculating.

CHAPTER 16

Build a Ladder

One important disadvantage to investing all bond assets in long-term bonds is that if a financial need arises, the investor might have to sell at a loss if interest rates have risen. Avoiding this by buying only short-term bonds exposes the investor to reinvestment risk, which means less income.

A LADDER APPROACH

To attain liquidity not readily available through long-term bonds and simultaneously minimize the effects of reinvestment risk, one can consider a variety of maturity dates, that is, use a "ladder" portfolio strategy. This approach involves investing in bonds with more than one maturity date; therefore a portion is always earning longer-term, higher rates. As each rung (bond) of the ladder matures, you reinvest the proceeds at the prevailing higher interest rate.

With the ladder portfolio, choose a maximum length of maturity, say five years. Then invest equal dollar amounts in bonds that mature at set intervals. It might be each year or every other year, obviously ending with the longest maturity. As a bond matures, it is reinvested into the next five-year bond.

INTEREST RATES

As inflation increases, the yield on the portfolio increases with each successive maturity and reinvestment. If interest rates go lower, the portfolio has a five-year hedge. With the average maturity at about three and one half years, interest rates won't affect bond prices much, and even if they do, it's not a long hold for maturity.

WHAT'S THE YIELD CURVE LOOK LIKE?

When investing in bonds, first check the yield curve. It dramatically illustrates the value of extended maturities. When inverted, it can suggest a lot about the probability of lower interest rates coming in the future.

The yield curve for January 15, 1999, shows a couple of inversions, but it is mostly flat to normal (Figure 16–1). This could be a concern, except that in this period it has been a relatively common appearance for the yield curve. The 30-year bond at 5.11% is 32 basis points (0.32%) lower than the 20-year bond and 97 basis points above the 1-year. Although that spread might tempt one toward the 30-year bond, keeping the objective of minimal risk to principal in mind, the investor establishes the ladder rungs.

ONE-YEAR TO FIVE-YEAR

With a $100,000 investment, the investor builds a five-year ladder.

Term	Amount	Yield (%)	Annual Income ($)
1 year	$20,000	4.46	892
2 years	$20,000	4.56	912
3-years	$20,000	4.70	940
4-years	$20,000	4.69	938
5-years	$20,000	4.76	952
Total	$100,000	4.6%	$4,634

ADVANTAGES AND DISADVANTAGES

The average yield of the bond portfolio is 4.6%, which is 14 basis points above the low and 16 basis points from the high. Many in-

Ladder, Yield Curve, January 15, 1999

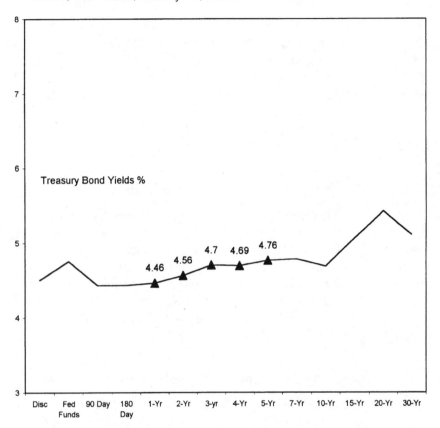

vestors might be tempted to hold off at this point to see if the yield curve would improve. The biggest problem with waiting for a better time is that it becomes too easy to remain a short-term investor.

An average annual yield of 4.6% might not be terribly exciting, but yield is not the only reason for using this strategy. The investor also wants to participate if rates increase. Every year, maturities will be reached and reinvested at prevailing rates. If the interest received is also reinvested, it will have a compounding effect and add income to each reinvestment. If interest rates go lower, the portfolio effectively has a five-year hedge. Predicting interest rates is always nearly impossible. With the ladder it's no longer necessary.

BUILDING THE LADDER

1. Select a Desirable and Practical Average Maturity.

The average maturity, whether 5 years, 10 years, or 20 years, should coincide with the length of time that the investor needs to receive highly predictable income from the portfolio. The amount of money available to invest can also be a factor. The ladder should have enough "rungs" so money can be reinvested every year or two. Longer reinvestment times could run the risk of missing interest rate changes. Most investors will do well with an average of between five and eight years.

2. Calculate the Longest Maturity to Be Used in the Portfolio

Assuming each bond is approximately equal in size (dollar amount invested) and they are spaced at even intervals, the longest-term instrument to be included should be about twice as long as the average term. An investor who determines that five years is an appropriate average term would use a 10-year security as the longest term in the fixed-income portfolio (2×5). If a five-year maximum maturity is more desirable, the ladder will have an average maturity of two and one-half years.

3. Select the Number of Rungs

Obviously, more rungs mean shorter intervals between maturity dates. Although several rungs can provide a smooth transition from one interest rate environment to another, too many positions can make reinvesting difficult and time-consuming.

4. Be Consistent

Each time an issue matures (every one or two years), the proceeds are to be reinvested at the longest maturity. If the investor desires to extend the average maturity, it can be done with each reinvestment by investing out six or seven years instead of five. Shortening the average can also be accomplished at reinvestment by buying shorter maturities. Just be careful that changes don't become irritatingly confused.

LADDER USE

Retirement

The investor can fund retirement accounts [IRA or 401(k)] for tax-deferred growth. Investors often use zero-coupon Treasuries or corporate zeros in a ladder. The zeros mature when the investor expects to have specific cash needs.

Education

Ladder portfolios can be constructed so they mature in August of each year to pay September tuition bills. Be careful with the timing on this; the exact timing of August is not as important as the year of maturity. Bond availability exactly timed to August might be a problem. If the bonds mature earlier, the funds can be put in a short-term certificate of deposit or money market account. Some investors begin ladders in their child's first year.

MIXED RUNG TYPES

The ladder can be used with Treasury bonds, corporate bonds, or a mixture. The investor is not limited to selecting only one type of bond. Selection of bond type should be based on the yield spread, the difference between the Treasury bond and corporate bond yield. If the 5-year Treasury is at 5% and an investment grade corporate bond (5-year maturity) is at 6.5%, the corporate bond could be the better selection for greater income. Mixing bonds with different risk levels can also be done, but care should be exercised to become well aware of the amount of risk being accepted. Determine how much damage will result if a higher-risk bond defaults.

INCOME FLEXIBILITY AND STABILITY

The greatest benefits of the ladder bond portfolio are flexibility and stability. Ladders create the stability of a steady income with the flexibility to follow interest rates. An additional advantage is low maintenance. With bonds maturing every year or two, it becomes a simple effort to reinvest in the next longest rung.

CHAPTER 17

Bonds, the Buy-and-Hold Investment

The case for buy-and-hold investing is strong with bonds, especially for individual investors. Whether it's coupon bonds that pay interest every six months or zero-coupon bonds that grow to face value, they could be described as investments designed for either income or growth. And the investor knows exactly how much money will be received in interest income and face value at maturity.

WITH COMMON STOCK, YOU DON'T KNOW

When an investor buys shares of common stock as an investment, there is no way to know whether it will be worth more or less in 10 years. Prices of stocks are influenced by a variety of economic, market, and performance factors. Some stocks pay dividends, but the dividends can change or be eliminated.

Stock investing always involves the question of how much will be earned over time. Stock prices move up, down, and sideways. If a price suffers a serious decline, the investor needs to make a decision regarding whether to sell and take a loss or hold for recovery. In the meantime, the declining price is eating away at the investor's profits and could eventually erode the principal.

BOND INCOME IS PRECISE

If a 10-year, 6% bond is purchased, the investor knows that 6% of the investment will be paid each year for 10 years and that the face value of the bonds will be returned at the end of the 10 years. It's the steady income, a known amount, that appeals to most investors.

Ten-Year Investment

Amount invested:	$100,000.00	
Number of bonds:	100	
Coupon of 6%:	$ 3,600.00	($1,800.00 every six months)
Total income:	$ 36,000.00	
Principal amount returned:	$100,000.00	

BOND PRICE CHANGES

For individuals, bond prices are important if one trades bonds. Also, prices can be important if it becomes necessary to sell some of the bonds to obtain cash. If the need for extra cash doesn't arise between purchase and maturity, price changes don't mean anything.

If the investor knows that a specific amount of cash will be needed in the next few months or in a couple of years, that amount should not be placed in long-term bonds. It can, however be invested in short-term bonds.

BOND RATING CHANGES

Bonds aren't without risk, although investment-grade bonds are lower risk than common stock. If a bond rating is downgraded by one of the rating agencies, it could be a signal of the possibility of default. Default occurs when the bond issuer is unable to make an interest payment and might not be able to make a repayment of principal.

Although bonds can be sold if they have been downgraded, this should be studied very carefully. A downgrade lowers the price significantly, so a current holder might have to sell at a loss of principal. Fortunately, it is usually only the lower-rated bonds that have much trouble. Although there have been situations where AAA and AA rated bonds have had problems, it is rare.

THEY'RE THE INCOME INVESTMENT

Bonds are meant to be income investments. Just as banks lend money to earn income, bonds allow an investor to earn income by lending money to governments, corporations, or other organizations.

CHAPTER 18

Bonds Lower
Portfolio Risk

Bonds can be a wonderful addition to an investment portfolio, the kind of addition that allows one to sleep better at night. The bonds provide steady income to be invested into other, possibly more speculative securities. Of course, this assumes the income is not needed for current living expenses.

AN OLD STRATEGY

An old investment strategy is for an investor to place all the investment money in coupon Treasury bonds and reinvest the interest payments into common stock. The principal is never at risk, assuming the bonds are held to maturity. Only the coupon payments become at risk when invested in the common stock.

If the common stock is carefully selected, the investor gets the best mix of growth and no risk to principal.

WHAT ABOUT ZERO-COUPON BONDS

A similar strategy can be implemented by using zero-coupon bonds. Since they don't make interest payments every six months (like coupon bonds), there is no maintenance necessary to reinvest.

If an investor has $100,000 to invest, he places half of the money in 100 zero-coupon treasury bonds that will mature in 12 years at 6%. At the end of the 12 years, the investor still has all of the principal investment of $100,000 (the face value of the zero coupon bonds at maturity) as well as whatever was gained by the $50,000 invested in stock.

Even if all was lost in the common stock, the investor still has the original principal of $100,000. Losing all of the principal invested in stock is a worst-case scenario that is not likely to occur. The strategy is particularly well-suited for retirement accounts where calculating the imputed tax is not necessary.

MIXED PORTFOLIO

Many investors keep it simple by investing long-term in some stock and some bonds. Whereas they are careful in their selection of stocks and bonds, they might not want to spend the time to perfectly balance a percentage of fixed income, common stock, and money market funds. They just invest in some stock and some bonds, depending on what looks attractive at the time they have the cash. The bonds will still lower the risk of the investment portfolio.

BONDS LOWER RISK IN THREE WAYS

Bonds lower the risk in an investment portfolio where some of the money is invested in stock.

1. *Principal is returned at maturity.* The only way stocks return the principal is if they are sold equal to or higher than the purchase price.

2. *Cash is paid out (coupon bonds) or interest is compounded (zero-coupon bonds).* The risk on any investment is lowered when cash is returned to the investor. This is also true of stocks that pay dividends. The risk is lowered by the amount paid. With the zero-coupon bond, it isn't paid out but is worked into the current discount price for the zero.

3. *Bonds are inherently lower-risk (than stocks) because of payment priority in the case of a corporate liquidation.*

CHAPTER 19

Calls Always Benefit the Issuer

The purpose of business is to make money. It is not to continue paying high bond yields when interest rates have dropped. Just as homeowners will refinance their mortgages when interest rates come down, corporations will call their high-interest bonds and reissue new bonds at lower yields.

CORPORATIONS WANT TO SELL BONDS

Whether interest rates are high or low, the majority of corporations must borrow money to stay in business. They might put a one-year or a five-year *no call* on their bonds. The purpose of the no call is to entice buyers. Buyers want to be able to lock in the highest possible yield, and the no-call says the bond cannot be called for the stated time.

Since the corporations cannot control what happens to interest rates, yet must borrow money to exist, they issue bonds with the idea of calling and refinancing when interest rates go lower. On the other hand, if interest rates rise further, they are not obligated to call the bonds and refinance.

FIGURE 19–1

Calls, AAA and BAA Corporate Bonds, 1988–1998

TEN YEARS OF DECLINING YIELDS

A chart of AAA and BAA bond yields from 1988 through 1998 shows clearly that interest rates can make significant moves in a short time (Figure 19–1).

The lower-rated BAA bonds hit a peak of 11.22% in August of 1988. From there, the yields dropped to 7.26% in 1993. That's nearly a 4% difference. It would save many companies millions of dollars. Homeowners will often refinance mortgages with only a 2% difference, sometimes even less. The AAA bonds dropped 3.63%, also a significant amount. There was a lot of bond calling and refinancing in those 10 years. Even many of the bonds issued in early September of 1992 were likely called when the one-year call protection expired.

Interest rates and bond yields seldom move in a straight line. In the fall of 1993, rates and yields moved up again. Within a year, the BAA bond yields moved up 2.07%, and the AAA 2.17%. As often happens, the rates peaked and dropped back down.

THE MAIN POINT

The point is, if corporations were forced to continue paying 10% or 11% when current yields are at 6% and 7%, it would stifle their ability to do business. One of the functions of higher interest rates is to slow business down in an overheating economy. When business slows, it becomes necessary to stimulate the economy with lowered interest rates. If companies were not able to call the high-interest bonds and issue new bonds at the lower yields, business and thereby the economy would not be stimulated.

A STRATEGY

A bond-investing strategy that became popular during the downtrend shown in Figure 19–1 was to buy long bonds with 1-year nocall, knowing they would be called. It made the long bond a short-term investment. This strategy will not work if the interest rates are rising, because the bonds obviously won't be called.

ASK ABOUT CALLS

When buying bonds, the investor should ask about the call and call protection, especially when interest rates are trending lower.

The Simplest Strategy

Buy the bullet and roll it
Anonymous

Bullet: The bullet is a bond with a maturity schedule that has the full payment of the principal on the final date the bonds are outstanding. An example of a bullet would be the $40,000,000 payment on January 20, 2000, on a $40,000,000 issue of bonds that matures in its entirety January 20, 2000. A bullet is also a form of term bond, which is a bond with a *single maturity date* (See Figure 20–1).

SIMPLER YET

Buy the 5-year Treasury note and roll it. In effect, it's like a bullet. Yieldwise, it's middle of the road investing, combining some of the best features of long- and short-term yields with the highest safety. It's an uncomplicated bond with a simple strategy.

30 YEARS, 6 BUYS

In June of 1968, the 10-year Treasury bond had a yield of only 5.72%. That was 13 basis points below the 5-year bond, a slight inversion at the time. The investor's average yield for the 30 years would have been 7.54%. Since the 5-year bond is a medium-term, it would have less price volatility risk than a 10- or 30-year bond. That could have been a big advantage if it was necessary to sell bonds for cash. The investor's yield increased as inflation was on the rise and decreased as inflation slowed. It was not usually the

F I G U R E 20–1

Buy the Bullet, 5-Year Treasury Bond, 1968–1998

highest yield (only during inversions), but it was never the lowest yield. Every five years, the investor received the principal back and reinvested.

LESS RISK

The lower risk is important. Of the Treasury bonds, the 5-year is probably the lowest risk for the highest return. There are times when the 5-year yield is higher than longer bond yields, i.e., when the yield curve inverts. There is still reinvestment risk; it can't be

F I G U R E 20–2

Yield Spread, 5-Year and 10-Year Treasury Bonds, 1968–1998

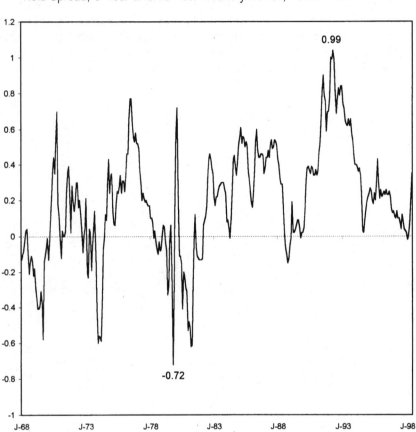

avoided. But to have to reinvest the principal every five years is neither a big risk nor a big task.

In the 30 years depicted, it is interesting that the highest possible 5-year yield was 15.93% and the lowest was 4.18%, a total spread of 11.75%. The example yield of 7.54% was half of the highest yield, and the high yield wasn't there for a long time.

When looking at the spread between the 5-year and 10-year bonds, it is interesting to see the amount of time the spread was negative. That means the 5-year had a higher yield than the 10-year bond (Figure 20–2).

MIDDLE OF THE ROAD

Many times, the middle course is the truest. The 5-year bullet can be as good as the 10-year bond and still have the advantages of less price volatility and an opportunity to lock in long-term if rates go high enough. It is the simple selection and can be good for either the bond investor or the asset allocation investor.

CHAPTER 21

Bond Investing Is Prudent Asset Allocation

The concept of asset allocation is not new. The basic idea is to spread investment over areas of high liquidity (money market), growth (common stock), and fixed-income (bonds). Asset allocation can be used to take advantage of the current investment climate, to moderate risk, or both.

The mix of bonds and stocks in an investment portfolio is the key to establishing effective and safe asset allocation. Bonds are considered the safety portion and common stock the risk portion of the portfolio. Although there can be many individual preferences for building an investment portfolio, here we will discuss just a few basic considerations.

ALLOCATION MIX CONSIDERATIONS

Age and Time Frame

The prevailing belief is that one can afford to take greater risk when young. Later, as one nears retirement, it becomes prudent to take less risk. The young investor has time to make up for losses. There are two difficulties with this belief. One is that too much risk is taken, and two, when a person is young, there aren't any assets to invest. However, the basic reasoning is sound. An investor with 20 or 25 years left to retirement can afford to take more risk than one who has only 5 or 10 years until retirement.

Market Conditions

As the investment climate becomes unfavorable with rising interest rates or market volatility, funds are shifted away from high-risk areas (common stock) to lower-risk investments like money markets and bonds. When the investment climate improves, the money is reallocated or rebalanced into investments with greater potential.

Aggressive strategies need to be especially careful of commissions, especially in volatile markets. Although brokerage firms like the commissions generated, an aggressive strategy doesn't necessarily improve the investor's return and often has only a minimal impact on market risk. If the economy experiences a sudden downturn with a bear market, both stock and bond prices will suffer.

Rebalance by Formula

Many investment firms have established formulas for the ideal balance. They might recommend an asset mix of 15% money market, 50% equities (common stock), and 35% fixed-income (bonds). If interest rates show signs of increasing, the rebalance might be 25% money market, 35% equities, and 40% fixed-income.

That's very nice, but in order to do the rebalance, an investor must sell stocks and buy bonds. Obviously, it would also be necessary to sell bonds and buy more stock when the investment climate improved. Some would debate the wisdom of such a speculative "market timing" approach in a conservative strategy.

Publicized Formulas

Many financial institutions and advisors publicize their recommended asset allocation mix based on current market conditions. Such information can be obtained from a stockbroker or by searching the keywords *asset allocation* on an Internet search engine. If checking on the Internet, be careful. Make certain the recommended mix has a recent date. It's also worthwhile to check more than one recommended mix, to get a feel for the different opinions.

Allocation by Risk

Asset allocation can strengthen safety with diversification and the inherent safety of bonds. The face value of the bonds is returned at maturity, and the risk is lowered with each six-month coupon payment.

A person's financial risk tolerance is a very personal and individual condition. People tend to have deep-seated fears about the worst happening to their money. That's why brokers and others selling financial products are so hesitant to discuss the risks involved.

Risk Aversive

A risk-aversive strategy might be to invest 75% in coupon bonds (you can make it even more risk aversive by placing that percentage in government bonds) and just 20% in stocks, with only a minimal 5% left for money market funds. As the bonds pay interest every six months, the funds can be used to buy more bonds or stock, depending on how it affects the balance.

Risk Moderate

Risk would be moderate with 50% of the funds in bonds, 45% in common stock, and 5% invested in money market funds. Again, the dividends can build up and be used to rebalance the portfolio.

Risk Aggressive

Although an investor may find aggressive investing an interesting strategy, some money in bonds adds a touch of prudence. It moderates the worst case scenario for the aggressive investor. If the worst happens to the stock portfolio, at least the bonds maintain some safety of principal. It might involve placing as little as 10% or 20% of the assets into bonds as a safety net. Care needs to be taken to rebalance and maintain the mix when the aggressive approach is successful.

The market value of the common stock can surge far ahead and skew the allocation percentages. If this happens, the investor should rebalance the portfolio to the original mix. If the initial plan called for 20% in bonds, keep it there, even if it becomes necessary to take some profits on the stock. This refers to maintaining the original set balance of the portfolio and not restructuring for market advantage.

INCOME NEEDS

Income needs now and estimated needs for the future are important when deciding on the asset mix. If an investor needs income

now, the amount of assets allocated for bond investing should obviously be higher than if income is needed 20 years from now.

PRUDENT INVESTING

Prudent investing sets an acceptable balance between risk and reward. Asset allocation using bonds can help the investor establish
and maintain a prudent investment portfolio. The safety isn't perfect. The risk cannot be eliminated. However it is moderated by the
safety of bonds over stocks.

CHAPTER 22

Pay Yourself First

**The first rule of investing is: Get some money.
The second rule of investing is: Don't lose it.**
Anonymous

In order to get some money and not lose it, an investor either inherits or works for money. Although the people who inherit money are often multiblessed, most people are not so fortunate. Most have to work for the money. But no matter how much or how little money a person is able to earn, it is always important to pay oneself first. It might be a significant amount of money or a modest amount, but the pattern needs to be established as soon as possible.

LIVE WITHIN YOUR MEANS

No, don't live within your means. Live below your means. Living within your means is spending every penny earned, and that's never a good habit to develop. It might be good for the federal government but not for individuals and families. Although living within one's means is better than living beyond one's means, it's not much better. If necessary, take a second job in order to have enough money to pay yourself first and have enough money left over for the basics and pleasantries. This can be especially effective when one is young, healthy, and has the energy to work two or more jobs.

Calculate and Set Spending Priorities

Write down monthly income. On a blank sheet of paper, write your monthly income. If your income is different every month, state it as an average or choose a lowest amount.

Pay Yourself First
Make a guesstimate as to how many dollars you think you will be able to pay yourself each month. Whether it's $500, $1000, or only $40 a month doesn't matter. What matters is the saving habit.

Use Windfalls as a Bonus
Many individuals can't wait to spend that small or large inheritance, bonus from work, or insurance settlement. It's a new VCR, stereo, or television set and poof, the money's spent and forgotten. If current debts are not burdensome, it might be better to borrow the money and make time payments. Use the windfall as an investment bonus.

Essential and Flexible Expenses
List monthly expenses, e.g., food, housing, utilities, transportation, loan payments, and insurance (if paid twice a year, divide by six). Then list flexible costs, such as credit card payments.

Nonessential Expenses
List elective spending, like restaurants, movies, or other forms of entertainment.

Calculate the Core Living Expense
Adding up the expenses will provide a dollar amount needed for every month. It is a core amount of money needed for survival. Subtract the amount from the monthly income. Hopefully, there will be some extra money. If the number is negative, either some trimming or another source of income is necessary.

Recalculate How Much to Pay Yourself
You might be able to pay yourself more than you initially believed. Be careful not to set the amount so high that it becomes impossible. It can easily lead to borrowing from savings for necessities, and that can quickly destroy the savings.

What About Setting a Budget?
Sure, if the budget is followed regularly. But checking and following a budget is something many people have trouble doing. A budget that is forgotten or ignored as soon as it is created becomes an exercise in futility. In many family and individual situations, a

carefully planned weekly grocery list will usually save more money than a detailed budget.

Pay Yourself Automatically

Whether it's by having a specific amount of money being automatically transferred to savings, to a retirement program at work, or sent to a mutual fund every month, paying yourself automatically is usually painless. It also tends to remove the temptation to spend any extra cash.

Saving and investing in the next millennium will become essential for retirement. The Social Security system could easily go the way of the horse and buggy or the railroads. Moving steadily away from debt and toward prudent investing could be the only strategy offering people a realistic chance for retirement.

CHAPTER 23

Be a Futures Hedger or a Speculator

In the arena of bond investing, one can be a speculator by buying and selling bonds. But there can be an irritating problem of getting current prices. Often, by the time a price is obtained, it changes. Another way to speculate on bonds is to trade futures or options traded on commodities exchanges.

CAUTION

A word of caution, the information presented here is brief. The investor should thoroughly study in-depth information on futures and options before investing. An excellent source of information is the Chicago Board of Trade (CBOT):

Chicago Board of Trade (CBOT)
141 West Jackson Boulevard
Chicago, IL 60604-2994
Phone: (312) 435-3500

WHAT IS A FUTURES CONTRACT?

A futures contract is an agreement to buy or sell a set amount of a commodity or financial instrument at a specific price at a date in the future. Futures prices are determined between buyer and seller on the floor (pits) of a commodity exchange, essentially using the open outcry system.

The contract obligates the futures buyer to purchase the underlying commodity or security and the seller to sell it unless the contract is sold before the settlement date. The futures contract differs from an option contract, in which the buyer can choose to exercise the option at any time before expiration. Futures contracts are standardized and meet the requirements of buyers or sellers for commodities and financial securities. Qualifications of quantity, quality, and delivery locations are well established. In a futures contract, the only variable is price. Price is "discovered" on the trading floor of an organized futures exchange through a process similar to an auction.

CBOT U.S. TREASURY FEATURES

U.S. Treasury Bond Futures Contract Specifications[1]

- Trading Unit: One U.S. Treasury bond having a face value at maturity of $100,000 or multiple thereof
- Deliverable Grades: U.S. Treasury bonds that, if callable, are not callable for at least 15 years from the first day of the delivery month or, if not callable, have a maturity of at least 15 years from the first day of the delivery month. The invoice price equals the futures settlement price times a conversion factor plus accrued interest. The conversion factor is the price of the delivered bond ($1 par value) to yield 8 percent.
- Price Quote: Points ($1000) and thirty-seconds of a point; for example, 80–16 equals $80^{16}/_{32}$.
- Tick Size: $^{1}/_{32}$ of a point ($31.25/contract); par is on the basis of 100 points
- Daily Price Limit: 3 points ($3000/contract) above or below the previous day's settlement price (expandable to 4½ points). Limits are lifted the second business day preceding the first day of the delivery month.
- Contract Months: March, June, September, December
- Delivery Method: Federal Reserve book-entry wire-transfer system

---

1 Information from Chicago Board of Trade, http://www.cbot.com/ourproducts/spec/
  spec10.htm. (Subject to change.)

- Last Trading Day: Seventh business day preceding the last business day of the delivery month

- Last Delivery Day: Last business day of the delivery month

- Trading Hours:

  Open outcry: 7:20 a.m.–2:00 p.m., Chicago time, Mon.–Fri.

  Project A®: Afternoon session 2:15–4:30 p.m., Chicago time, Mon.–Thu.

  Overnight session: 6:00 p.m.–5:00 a.m., Chicago time, Sun.–Thu.

  Day session: 5:30 a.m.–2:00 p.m., Chicago time, Mon.–Fri.

  Trading in expiring contracts closes at noon on the last trading day.

- Ticker Symbol: Open Outcry: US

- Project A®: ZB

HEDGING

Hedging is one of the main uses of a futures contract. It is the buying or selling of futures contracts for the purpose of offsetting the risk of changing prices in the cash markets. Futures contracts can be used to hedge currencies, stock indexes, government bonds, and other financial instruments.

If an investor holds Treasury bonds and wants to take advantage of the current market, futures can be sold on the Treasuries. In a few months, when the bond market falls, the investor sells the Treasury bonds at a loss but buys Treasury bond futures, offsetting the earlier sell. The futures profit protects against the loss. Hedging, in its simplest form, is offsetting price risk by taking an equal but opposite position in the futures market. The hedger's objective is primarily to protect investments rather than make additional profits.

SPECULATOR DEFINED

What is a speculator? In the futures markets, there are speculators and hedgers. Both are essential for the markets to exist. The speculators are investors willing to accept the risk that hedgers are trying to avoid. Motivated by profits, speculators assume risk and provide the futures markets with the necessary liquidity for active trading. When the speculators are correct, they make a profit. When they are wrong, they supply cash.

SPECULATOR TRADING TYPES

Speculators are classed by the three trading methods they use: position traders, day traders, and scalpers.

Position Traders

The position trader initiates a futures or option position and holds it for a period of time (days, weeks, or months).

Day Traders

As the name suggests, the day trader holds futures or options positions only during the trading day. Most are futures exchange members executing trades in the trading pits.

Scalpers

Professional futures and options traders who trade for their own accounts in the trading pits are known as scalpers. Their strategy is to make small profits or losses on many trades. They have a willingness to buy at the bid price and sell at the ask, or offer, price, thereby helping to make the market highly liquid. Scalpers are also day traders; they will seldom hold a position overnight.

SPECULATORS STILL MANAGE RISK

Speculators set maximum acceptable losses, either as a percentage or a specific dollar amount, and have the discipline to stay with them. They make use of stop-loss orders and do not lower them. Buy-stop orders are never raised.

Risk is further managed by diversification in different futures markets. Speculators have a set plan that is followed. In the plan, they decide on the amount of loss they are willing to take and on the amount of expected gain. They stay with their own ideas rather than letting the opinions of others persuade them away from their plan. They are willing to close out a losing position. They know precisely how much money should be at risk and stay with the amount. They remain cool in difficult times and never add to a losing position.

IT'S ANOTHER WORLD

The terminology is different. The variations are different. But the motivations for trading futures are similar to other areas of investing: to minimize losses or maximize returns. That's what futures trading is all about.

CHAPTER 24

Buy Inflation Protection Bonds

On Wednesday, January 29, 1997, the United States Treasury made its first issue of an inflation-linked bond, the 3.375% of 2007. Essentially, the new bond, Treasury Inflation Protection bonds (called TIPs) increases its principal according to changes in the Consumer Price Index (CPI). Its interest payment is calculated on the inflated bond principal, which is eventually repaid at maturity. The bond gives an investor the ability to protect against inflation while providing a certain "real" return over an investment horizon.

COMPARE TO "REGULAR" TREASURY

The value of the inflation protection of the TIPS was actively debated in many investment circles. How does it compare to a normal Treasury bond? We can compare the yield available on a regular 10-year Treasury bond to the TIP yield. At the time of issue, current yields on a regular 10-year Treasury were 6.4%. If we subtract inflation, currently 3.3% for the Consumer Price Index (CPI), we get a "real yield" of 3.1% (6.4 – 3.3 = 3.1). If the current yield of the TIPS is 3.3% "real," it means the real yield of the TIPS is 0.2% higher than a regular Treasury of the same term.

CPI DEBATE

For some time a debate has raged about the Consumer Price Index, many claiming it is overstated by as much as 1.5%. The big question with TIPS then becomes, if the CPI is corrected, will the bonds be lowered also? As it stands now, they probably will be dropped accordingly.

The CPI situation needs to be dealt with and firmly set if bonds like TIPS are to continue being attractive to investors. Otherwise, the bonds might never develop a trading market and could go the way of the silver dollar, eventually disappearing from lack of interest.

TIPS ARE INFLATION INSURANCE

Inflation, although it has been remarkably under control for the past five years at 3% plus or minus, is the largest threat a fixed-income investor faces. But by 1998, many bond managers and investors were beginning to believe higher inflation would not return. Compare this to the ravaged bond investors of the 1970s, who referred to bonds as "certificates of confiscation." The climate now has bond managers wanting 100-year securities and fretting about bond shortages.

WRONG TIME

Is there a wrong time to buy inflation-protected bonds? At least one noteworthy economist makes the point.

> Sung Won Sohn, economist for Norwest Corp. in Minneapolis, said the wrong time to buy such bonds would have been the early 1980s. As interest rates plummeted, investors wouldn't have gotten an extra kick pegged to inflation.[1]

Sohn went on to suggest that individual investors consider putting 10% to 15% of their bond portfolios in the new bonds as an inflation-hedge.

---

1 Susan Tompor, "Indexed to Inflation, New Treasury Bonds May Put Your Fears About Future to Rest," *The Detroit News,* May 30, 1996, http://www.detnews.com/menu/stories/50107.htm.

DIFFERENT FROM SHORT-TERM BONDS

Buying short-term bonds effectively adjusts for inflation and leaves the opportunity open to buy long-term if interest rates and yields get high enough. So how is the TIPS opportunity better?

- There is no need to reinvest funds.
- Effectively a 10-year yield in any inflationary trend because the bond is adjusted to inflation.

Therefore, TIPs should do better than following rates up with short-term investing.

WAVE OF THE FUTURE

Although there are questions to be settled regarding the accuracy of the Consumer Price Index and the liquidity for buying and selling TIPs, the bonds stand an excellent chance to be the debt wave of the future. That could bring a new question to the front. When TIPs become the "regular" Treasury bond, how will it change the texture of the economy? Nevertheless, for individual investors, TIPs now provide an alternative bond with an inflation protection benefit.

Buy Stocks with Bonds (Convertibles)

A convertible bond is one that can be changed into the issuing company's common stock. The option to convert the bond is determined by the investor. Conversion ratios, the number of shares per bond, are set by the company. The terms of conversion are set forth in a *bond indenture,* which defines the exact number of shares or the method of determining how many shares per bond will be received. For instance, a bond might say that it is convertible into 20 shares, making the conversion ratio 20 to 1.

Although that's the basic explanation, unfortunately, it's usually not so easy. The indenture can also state a conversion price, the price per share at which the company is willing to trade shares of stock for the bond. If the conversion price is $100 per share, the bond is convertible into 10 shares of stock. (Divide the face value (normally $1000) by the set conversion price.)

RATIO CHANGES

If set forth in the indenture, a conversion ratio can change through the years. It might be $100 for the first five years, $110 for the next five years, and so forth. To minimize a lowering of the value of the existing stock, there are also antidilution provisions with the conversion feature. If the common stock were to split 3 for 1 and the conversion ratio was 10 to 1 prior to the split, after the split, the conversion ratio would be 30 to 1. A stock dividend would have a similar effect. Obviously, a stock split also reduces the conversion price by the amount of the split.

COST OF THE EXTRA BENEFIT

Convertible bonds have a something extra, that being the right to convert to common stock. The bondholder pays for the extra benefit by having to accept a slightly lower interest rate. The price of the common stock also influences the bond price. If the stock price rises, the bond price increases.

CALLABLE FEATURE

Most convertible bonds are callable. The company can force the conversion by calling the bonds (*forced conversion*). When a bond is converted to common stock, corporate debt is reduced as debt becomes equity (ownership).

OWNERSHIP DILUTION

Converting bonds (debt) into common stock (equity) dilutes the equity. The company didn't grow larger with the additional stock. Instead, each stockholder's piece of ownership became smaller.

TRADING AT PARITY

Another important term is *parity*. If the $1000 bond is convertible into 10 shares of stock, the parity stock price is $100. If the stock price rises to $150, for the stock and bonds to be at parity, the bonds will trade at $1500.

INVESTOR BENEFITS

Investors buy convertible bonds to have current income and less downside risk. The convertible should trade to its bond value if there is a severe drop in the common share price. Investors often use *break-even analysis* to compare the coupon payment of the convertible bond to the dividend yield of the common stock shares. The investor can stay with the bond and its coupon income while waiting for the stock price to improve.

CHAPTER 26

Beware the GNMA

The Government National Mortgage Association, nicknamed the GNMA, or Ginnie May, is essentially another form of government bond. Strictly speaking, it is a government agency (a govie) bond that is also called a *mortgage-backed (pass-through) security*. In effect, it is the reverse of a home mortgage. GNMAs are fully guaranteed by the United States government as to payment of interest and principal. Although many government agency securities have such a guarantee implied, they don't all have the direct guarantee like the GNMA. Several mortgages are bundled together to form a GNMA pool. The investor buys a part of a specific mortgage pool.

THE MOST MISUNDERSTOOD POINT

The GNMA makes monthly payments, just as a homeowner makes monthly payments on a mortgage. When the homeowner makes a payment, part is interest and part is principal. When the investor receives the monthly payment, part is interest and part is principal. The money (interest and principal) goes from the homeowner to the investor and "passes through" the Government National Mortgage Association. What this means is that unlike a Treasury bond or corporate bond, which returns the principal at maturity, principal is being returned in the monthly payments.

The difference is important. It is often misunderstood by GNMA investors, who sometimes are not aware that part of their

monthly payment is principal, or they forget. Instead, they believe
the payments all to be part of the bond yield. When the GNMA matures or closes out, these investors have the unpleasant surprise of
not understanding where their principal money has gone. They
have been receiving it all along.

REINVEST THE PRINCIPAL

The investor must therefore make other arrangements to reinvest
the principal, possibly holding the funds in money market or other
short-term securities until enough cash is accumulated to buy another GNMA or other security. Although some dislike dealing with
the return of principal on a monthly basis, others view it as a way
to participate in interest rate increases by reinvesting short-term,
thereby creating a modest inflation hedge.

WHAT ABOUT SAFETY

The GNMA is specifically backed by the full faith and credit of the
United States government as to payment of interest and principal.
That means they are virtually as safe as direct obligation Treasury
bonds.

GNMAs are bought and sold in a highly liquid market. The
prices fluctuate as with other bonds. If interest rates rise, the existing GNMA price goes down. If interest rates drop, the existing
GNMA price goes up. The GNMA has another risk similar to a
callable bond. Homeowners are constantly refinancing their mortgages, especially when interest rates go lower. Mortgages are also
paid off and new ones issued when homeowners sell and move.
When a mortgage is paid off, the principal is paid back to GNMA
and ultimately to the investor. In other words, the 30-year GNMA
doesn't normally last for the full 30 years.

GNMA ADVANTAGES

Unlike most bonds, the GNMA pays monthly instead of every six
months. The interest rates on GNMAs tend to run a percentage
point or two above comparable Treasury bonds. GNMA interest
and principal payments are backed by the U.S. government.

Put Compound Interest to Work with Zeroes

When zero-coupon bonds became available, many people were confused. Why would they want a bond without coupon payments every six months? For many years, bonds meant regular interest payments. Why is it better to get all the interest at once? Designed for investors who don't need the current income, zeroes have two big advantages. First, the investor doesn't have the six-month coupon payment to worry about reinvesting. Second, the interest compounds; it pays interest on interest.

COUPON DIFFERENCE

A few years ago, a new bond had several coupons attached. Bondowners would take a scissors to the bond, clip out the coupon, and present it to the bond issuer or to a bank for payment. Usually this was necessary every six months. Those were called *bearer bonds*, meaning the person with physical possession of the bond (the bearer) was the owner. Now, bonds are issued as *registered*, which means that even if an investor can't physically hold the actual bond (book-entry), it will be registered in the investor's name and interest will be mailed every six months. This removes all the coupon-handling headaches for both the issuer and the bondowner. Also, when held in book-entry, it is less likely that the bonds will be stolen or damaged. Although there aren't any paper coupons to clip, bonds that pay out cash interest every six months are still called coupon bonds.

When the bond matures, the issuer redeems the bond and pays an owner the face amount. The holder may have paid $1000 for the bond and received cash interest payments every six months for 20 years. The investor redeems the matured bond for $1000 face value.

ZERO COUPON

A zero-coupon bond has no coupons, and there is no interest paid out. However, at maturity, the issuer redeems the bond at face value. Obviously, the original cost discount of a $1000 bond is much less than $1000. The difference between the face value and the amount of money paid for the bonds is compound interest.

The market price depends on:

1. The holding period, i.e., the number of years to maturity
2. The current interest rates
3. The risk involved (with the bond issuer).

TAXES

Even though the bondholder does not receive any interest income while holding zeroes, in the United States the IRS requires that a zero-coupon owner "impute" an annual interest income and report the income each year. Usually, the issuer will send an investor a Form 1099-OID (original issue discount), which shows the imputed interest. Also, an IRS publication explains imputed interest on original issue discount instruments.

CAPITAL GAINS

For capital gains purposes, the imputed interest earned between the time the bond is acquired and the time it is sold, or redeemed, is added to the cost basis. If the owner holds the bond continually from the time issued until it matures, there will generally not be any capital gain or loss.

Zeroes tend to be more susceptible to changing interest rates. Some people buy zeroes hoping to get capital gains when interest rates drop. If rates go up, they can always hold them to maturity without any loss.

IDEAL FOR IRA ACCOUNT

Zeroes sometimes pay better yields than coupon bonds. When a zero is in a tax-deferred account such as an IRA, the imputed interest does not have to be reported.

SOURCES AND FORMS

Essentially, zero-coupon bonds are available from the same sources as registered coupon bonds. The federal government, its agencies, municipalities, and corporations market zero-coupon bonds. In some situations, coupon bonds have been converted into zeroes. Some financial products combine zeroes and regular coupon bonds. For example, a bond may be a zero for the first five years of its life and pay a set coupon interest rate thereafter. It will be treated as an OID instrument while it pays no interest.

ZEROES CAN BE CALLABLE

Like other bonds, some zeroes are callable by the issuer prior to maturity at a stated call price. Obviously, they can also have a no-call period.

DEEP DISCOUNT

Instead of paying coupon interest every six months, zeroes are bought at a deep discount to their value at maturity (face value). A bond that pays a face value of $100,000 when it matures in 25 years could cost $17,500 currently. The return for the 25 years would amount to just over 7.22% per year. The percentage here is a yield to maturity (YTM) and is an important consideration when investing in zeros.

HOW FAST DOES IT GROW?

Based on compound interest rates alone, these bonds would be worth $35,141.83 in 10 years, $49,798.66 in 15 years, $70,568.49 in 20 years, and, of course, the full $100,000 in 25 years.

HOW DOES IT COMPARE TO A COUPON BOND?

The total income from the zero coupon bond would be $82,500.92. If the same $17,500 were invested in a coupon bond that paid money out every six months, the total income would only be $30, 625, a difference of $51,875.92. How can this be such a big difference? With the zero, the lender has the use of the money for 25 years, whereas with the coupon bond, money is being paid out. That fact also means the zero is inherently riskier than the coupon bond, whose risk is lowered with each interest payment.

BENEFITS

One benefit of the zero bonds is that the investor knows exactly what will be returned if the bond is held until it matures. In this example, it is $100,000. Another important benefit is that the investor doesn't have to reinvest coupon payments every six months.

DRAWBACKS

The drawback is that if an investor is locked into a zero with a yield to maturity of 7.22%, an increase in interest rates could mean better is available elsewhere. This is a similar problem with all long-term bonds.

Another major concern with zeroes is price volatility, which is greater than with coupon bonds. If interest rates rise, the market price of these bonds can fall dramatically, although price volatility is usually only a problem if the bonds have to be sold before they mature and yields have risen. If yields have fallen, the price of zeroes rises, and they can be profitable if sold early.

ALL POINTS CONSIDERED

The zero-coupon bond can be useful in most investment portfolios, but it is especially convenient for retirement investment accounts where the investor does not want cash to deal with every six months. Although they can provide some excellent capital gains if bond yields have fallen, zeroes should be considered a long-term investment.

CHAPTER 28

Understand the Indexes

People in the United States and much of the world see on television or hear radio reports about the daily movement of the Dow Jones Industrial Average. They might hear that the Dow set a new record high, or that it dropped nearly 300 points. People tend to believe that up is good for the economy and down is bad. Many do not understand what the Dow is or how it is constructed.

The Dow Jones Industrial Average is a market index formed from the stock prices of 30 companies that are believed to be representative of the market. More accurately, it is a simple average, calculated by adding up all the stock prices and dividing by a special divisor. The divisor takes into account changes by stock splits and dividends.

DEFINING THE DOW

The Dow Jones Industrial Average is the oldest and most frequently quoted market index, dating back to 1884. Founding father of Dow Jones & Company and *The Wall Street Journal*, Charles Dow assembled a list of closing prices of 11 stocks. The prices and other investing information were published in a financial bulletin as well as the financial newspaper he established with his partners Edward D. Jones and William Bergstresser.

BLUE CHIPS

Today, the Dow Average is composed of 30 major corporations. The stocks are often called *blue-chip stocks*, and include such companies as IBM, General Motors, 3-M, AT&T, and other well-known large corporations. Often simply referred to as "the Dow," it is effectively a price-weighted index (stocks are accorded relative importance based on their prices). Because it is an average, higher-priced stocks have stronger impact on the index than lower-priced stocks.

Some analysts believe the Dow is no longer representative of the broad market, partly because the 30 companies represent less than 15% of the current market value of the stocks traded on the New York Stock Exchange.

Two broader market indexes have gained popularity among analysts, the Standard & Poor's 500 Composite Stock Price Index and the Wilshire 5000 Index.

STANDARD & POOR'S 500 INDEX

The S&P 500 Index includes an estimated 69% of the market value of the U.S. stock market, although it is still dominated by larger companies. The index is made up of 378 industrial, 47 utility, 59 financial, and 16 transportation issues. The S&P 500 is a true index, meaning it is market-weighted. The stocks are weighted according to the total market value of their outstanding shares. Each stock influences changes in the Index in proportion to its size, not just its price.

THE WILSHIRE 5000 INDEX

The Wilshire 5000 Index includes securities regularly traded on the New York Stock Exchange and the American Stock Exchange. Also, it includes the NASDAQ (over-the-counter) stocks. The index has grown and is now made up of more than 6000 companies' stocks and is essentially an overall market measure for U.S. stocks.

LEHMAN BROTHERS AGGREGATE BOND INDEX

The Lehman Brothers Aggregate Bond Index, representing 6000 high-quality corporate, government, and mortgage-backed securities, is a popular benchmark for investment-grade bonds. Narrowly

focused bond indexes also exist. They are normally based on particular quality and maturity characteristics.

OTHER BOND INDEXES

Lehman Brothers Government Bond Index: Tracks U.S.
government agency and Treasury bonds.

Lehman Brothers Corporate Bond Index: Tracks fixed-rate,
nonconvertible, investment-grade corporate bonds.

Lehman Brothers Mortgage-Backed Securities Index: Tracks
fixed-rate securities of the Government National Mortgage
Association (GNMA), the Federal National Mortgage
Association (FNMA), and Federal National Loan
Mortgage Corporation (FHLMC).

WHAT ARE INDEXES FOR?

Indexes have two primary uses.

1. They serve as a benchmark for the performance of an
   investment advisor or other stock or bond portfolio
   manager. If a manager performs better than the index,
   great rewards ensue. If the index does better, the manager
   looks for a new job.
2. Indexes are used by analysts as an indicator of the current
   strength in the market or a market segment. For the
   technical analyst, the index can also give a sense of
   direction and a signal of possible change. Is the trend
   firmly advancing or showing weakness and about to
   turn?

INDEX FUNDS

Index funds for stocks have been around for the last decade or
more, but in the last few years, index funds for bonds have also become popular. If an investor wants to match the performance of the
Standard & Poor's 500 Index, why not just buy a mutual fund
based on the index? With bonds, why not set up a fund to match
the Lehman Brothers Aggregate Bond Index? Matching a benchmark index is a simple approach, perhaps too simple. Indexes

weighted to the number of outstanding securities would be impossible to match. In the S&P 500 Index, all the shares of every company are accounted for, that would obviously be impossible in a fund.

INDEXES AROUND THE WORLD

During the past few years, exchanges around the world have been working to upgrade their images, fair practices, and integrity of operations. Most have developed some kind of "all shares" fund and are working on the development of indexes with specific focal points. Indexes give them a way to measure the progress of their markets and will eventually bring them more trading business.

FOR THE INDIVIDUAL

Follow the progress of two or three indexes to look for signals of strength or weakness in the market. Follow the trends. Look for places where the trendline is broken and possibly signaling a change of direction (see Chapter 30 regarding trends).

CHAPTER 29

Do the Barbell

Here you have the best of both worlds, high yields on one end and moving yields on the other. A bond strategy similar to the ladder (Chapter 16) but simpler in some ways is to buy the "barbell" to keep some money short-term, yet still take advantage of higher yields in long-term money.

Divide your assets allocated for bonds into two parts. The money can be divided equally or more at one end than the other, but only into two parts. It would seem logical to have more short-term if interest rates are relatively low. Keep the amounts equal if interest rates are stable. Have more in long-term if interest rates are on the high side. That's a matter of finesse. Here we will keep the amounts equal. An investor with $100,000 to invest could put $50,000 into long bonds and $50,000 into short-term bonds.

CHECK THE YIELD CURVE

First, look at the yield curve. Is the yield curve normal, steep, flat, or inverted? What's the spread between the short-term and long-term bonds?

EXAMPLE, 1978–1998

Look at the yield curve back in January of 1978 (Figure 29–1). It appears to be normal. The high yields are long-term and the low yields are short-term. The spread between the 1-year and 30-year bonds is 0.92% (92 basis points).

F I G U R E 29–1

Yield Curve, U.S. Treasury Bonds, January 25, 1978

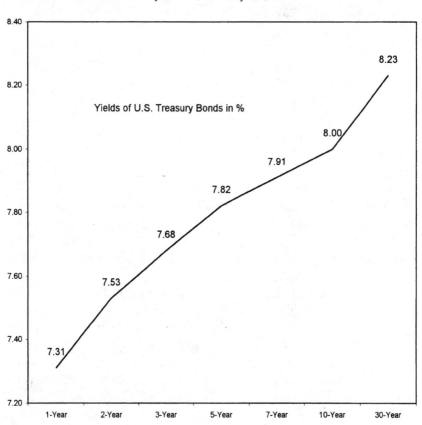

DO THE BARBELL

An investor with $100,000 decides to buy $50,000 of 1-year and
$50,000 of 30-year Treasury bonds:

Bonds	Description	Current Yield	Annual Income
50	1-year Treasury bonds	7.31%	$3655
50	30-year Treasury bonds	8.23%	$4115
100	First-year total annual income		$7770
	First-year average yield	7.70%	

The first-year average yield is only 0.39% (39 basis points) away from the highest 30-year yield, yet the investor has $50,000 that will mature in a year. The funds will be good protection if interest rates rise.

WHAT HAPPENED?

Figure 29–2 illustrates what happened with the investor keeping the barbell intact. Each year, a new 1-year U.S. Treasury bond was purchased. The dotted line on the chart shows the average yield from 1978–1998.

FIGURE 29–2

Barbell Average Yield, 1978–1998

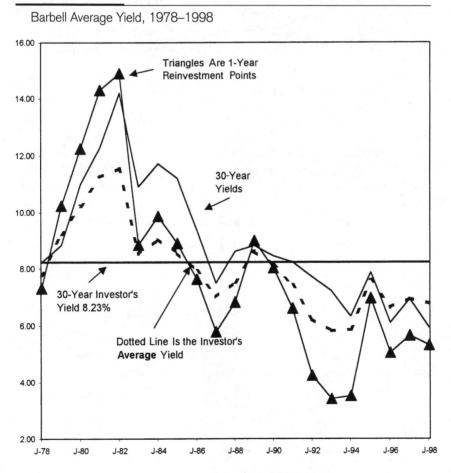

The straight line represents the investor's purchase of a 30-year bond at a yield of 8.23%. Tracking of 30-year bond yields is also included for reference.

The investor ran right into the inverted yield curve of the 1980s and did very well with the 1-year yields being higher than the 30-year yields. The example illustrates a big advantage to the barbell strategy. Investing in the 1-year bonds became a big advantage in the mid-1980s, bringing in extra cash with higher yields.

The time shown here is ideal because it clearly illustrates what happens to the barbell when interest rates go up and when they drop. The short-term bonds help the average yield as interest rates rise, and the long-term bonds help maintain the average as interest rates fall.

Notice how the investor's average yield rises above the going rate on 30-year yields in the mid-1990s and remains higher through 1998. First, it's pulled up by the high short-term yields and later by the yield on the 30-year bond initially purchased by the investor.

CONSERVATIVE STRATEGY

Actually, the barbell is a more conservative strategy than just buying a long-term bond and holding it to maturity. It has the advantage of moderating the risk of rising interest rates, with the extra benefit of allowing the investor to partially partake of the higher yields. With bonds maturing every year, it lowers the risk of the investor having to take a loss by selling when interest rates have risen. Short-term bond prices are not as volatile as the long-term prices.

CHAPTER 30

Do Bond
Market Analysis

Many individuals select bonds as their investment of choice because they consider them the "buy and forget" investment. For analysis, they simply stay with government or investment grade (BBB or better) and check the yield curve for the maturity that best fits their needs. They may check the current trend in interest rates to see if it's up or down, but that's about all. Buy the bonds and let the income roll in every six months. Essentially, these investors are analyzing the bonds on a fundamental and technical analysis level, without looking into the economic forces behind the bonds.

FUNDAMENTAL ANALYSIS

Looking into the fundamentals of the economy or of a specific company to draw conclusions based on business growth is what fundamental analysis is all about. Keeping up with business news to know if the leading economic indicators show the economy to be contracting or expanding can inform the investor of possible recession or prosperity ahead.

Tracking the Consumer Price Index (Chapter 40) to see if inflation remains in an "acceptable" range or is escalating can help the investor decide if now is a good time to buy bonds of long- or short-term maturities.

Market traders and analysts tend to follow all economic indicators as the figures are released to the news distribution media. Their reaction to a news release is often not based directly on the information but on how the information compares to their expectations. They pay especially close attention to inflation, bond prices (and yields), the stock market, and all the other economic indicators.

ECONOMIC INDICATORS

The three main classes of monthly economic indicators are:

Leading: On the leading edge of economic growth
Coincident: Moving with the economic growth
Lagging: Following the economic growth

Ten of the most closely watched leading indicators are:[1]

1. Average work week, production workers' hours
2. Average weekly initial claims, state unemployment insurance
3. Manufacturers' new orders, consumer goods and materials
4. Vendor performance—slow deliveries diffusion index
5. Manufacturers' new orders, nondefense capital goods
6. Building permits
7. Stock prices, 500 common stocks
8. Money supply, M2
9. Interest-rate spread, 10-year Treasury bonds less Fed-Funds
10. Index of consumer expectations

Figure 30–1 shows three years' worth of leading indicator behavior.

Four common coincident indicators are:

1. Employees on nonagricultural payrolls
2. Personal income less transfer payments
3. Industrial production
4. Manufacturing and trade sales

---

1 Economic indicator information can be obtained at the Internet site of The Conference Board, www.tcb-indicators.org.

F I G U R E 30–1

Index of Leading Economic Indicators, 1995–1998

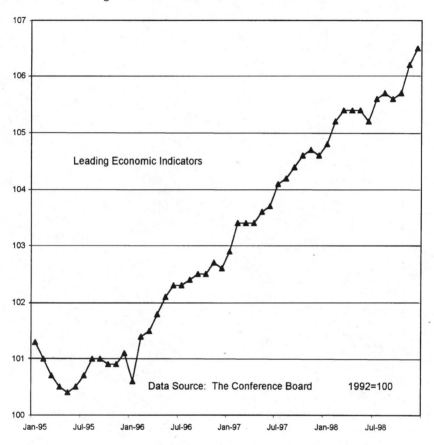

The index is shown in Figure 30–2.

Among lagging indicators are the following seven (see Figure 30–3):

1. Average duration of unemployment
2. Ratio, manufacturing and trade inventories to sales
3. Change in index of labor cost per unit of output, manufacturing
4. Average prime rate charged by banks
5. Commercial and industrial loans
6. Ratio, consumer installment credit outstanding to personal income
7. Change in Consumer Price Index for services

F I G U R E 30–2

Index of Coincident Economic Indicators, 1995–1998

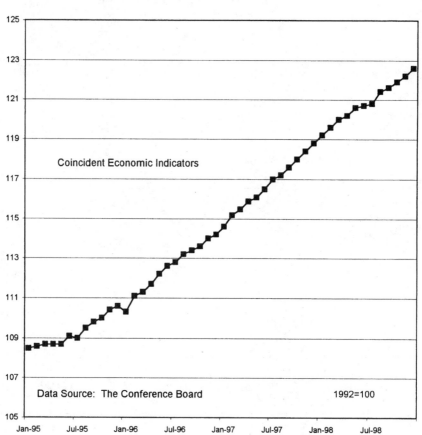

INDEXES RELEASED LATER

Each economic indicator index can be referenced; however, information on the components is released before their respective index, which is more of a composite. Current analysis is generally done on the components rather than on the later index release. The indexes do give a good perspective on economic growth when placed on a chart. Generally, if the leading indicators decline for three consecutive months, it is believed to forecast a recession. The amount of time between any forecast and an actual recession can

F I G U R E 30–3

Index of Lagging Economic Indicators, 1995–1998

Data Source: The Conference Board   1992=100

vary greatly because of efforts taken to prevent the economic slump.

HELP-WANTED ADVERTISING INDEX

Another leading indicator many analysts follow is the Help-Wanted Advertising Index. It is usually compared to 3-month U.S. Treasury bills (Figure 30–4).

You can see the index line turn before the T-bill yields line, but what does it mean? Really, if the want ads go up before the T-bill

F I G U R E 30–4

Leading Indicator, Help-Wanted Index and 3-Month Treasury-Bill Yields

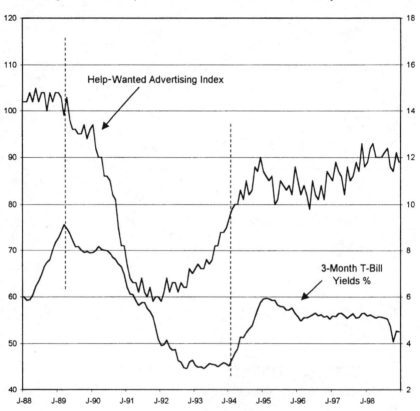

yields, does it mean inflation is coming? And when the want ads decrease in number, does it mean companies aren't doing any hiring because they believe they won't be able to afford paying the new employees? Although it's difficult to decipher what's really going on, one thing obvious is that the Help-Wanted Advertising Index appears to turn before T-bill yields.

THE FED

Professional traders will track changes in all of the economic indicators. They will also try to forecast what the Federal Reserve Bank will do with interest rates. In fact, they must make two forecasts, what the Fed will do and how the market will react.

FIGURE 30–5

Rates and Yields, 1982–1998

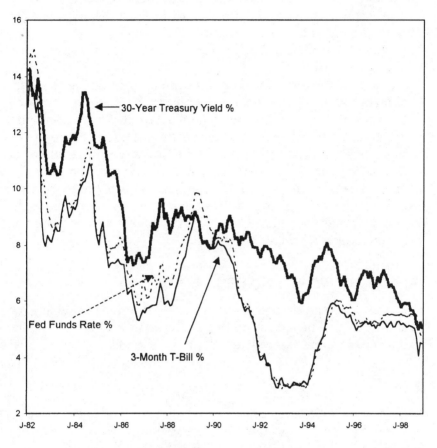

A chart of the fed funds interest rate, 3-month T-bill, and 30-year Treasury yields shows that the fed funds has some forecasting reliability for the short-term (Figure 30–5). Fed funds tend to turn before bond yields. Even so, it should never be the only indicator followed.

Indicators, whether they are fundamental or technical, can send false signals or mixed signals. With a false signal, either nothing happens in the markets or the markets make only a small adjustment that is back to the previous trend within a few trading sessions. Mixed signals between indicators can cause market volatility.

TECHNICAL ANALYSIS

The study of economics and market movements is never an exact science, especially when attempting to forecast. Many analysts, traders, and individuals in the bond markets will rely on both fundamental analysis and technical analysis, while a few purists focus only on the technicals.

Fundamental analysis looks at information affecting the markets. Technical analysis is nearly the opposite; it looks at the market's reaction in order to forecast where the market might be going next. Again, technical analysis is imprecise. It's more an attempt to understand the thinking of the trading crowd. Technical analysts tend to focus on price movements, trading volume, and open interest (short-selling information). The belief is that the market reflects the sum total of all available economic information relating to the markets. It's more based on what is happening with prices rather than on what might happen.

TRENDS, SUPPORT, AND RESISTANCE

Technical analysis looks at charts. Prices, interest-rate levels, or yields are plotted on a chart, with trendlines drawn to show the direction and to some extent strength of movements.

TRENDS

A trend remains in force until a trend changes. Change is usually signaled by the penetration of a trend line. Uptrend lines are drawn on the underside of the "sawtooth" fluctuation points, and downtrend lines are drawn on the top of the points. Exact placement is a matter of continual debate among analysts. Some say place trend lines at the most extreme points; others say find the fit where the line hits the greatest number of points. Obviously, the difference between these two locations can be a considerable distance. Using only extremes can miss many "secondary trends." Using a "best-fit" approach shows secondary trends and previous trend line violations where a turn did not occur.

Looking at the 3-month T-bill chart (Figure 30–6) shows the yields penetrating the trend line several times before the end of August. In August yields broke through the trend line and much farther. They dropped 1.40% (140 basis points). Keep in mind that

F I G U R E 30–6

Trend, Support, Resistance, 3-Month Yields, 1998–1999

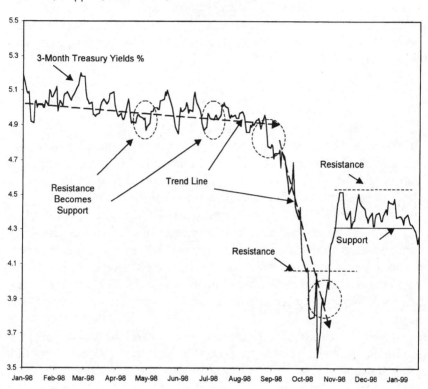

the drop of yields means buyers. Investors were buying up short-term T-bills, probably fearing the possibility of higher interest rates. As the fears dissipated, the T-bills were sold and rates moved up to a modestly higher level.

Support

Support is a level where the line stops dropping and goes back up. In the stock market, support is defined as the price or index level where buyers enter the market. With bond yields, it would be the point where sellers appear and yields rise as bond prices drop. A support line can be the same as a trend line or it can be drawn separately, nearly horizontal.

Strong support is where the moving price or yield line comes down and touches support several times. When the moving line breaks through support, support converts to resistance. The "breakout" to the downside is usually considered a signal of weakness in the stock market. Again, with bond yields dropping, it's a sign of buyers.

Resistance

Resistance is the level where an upward moving line stops and drops back. In the stock market, resistance is the point where sellers come into the market. In the bond market, a chart showing yields would have resistance at the point where buyers enter, thereby pushing yields lower and prices higher. Resistance can be drawn as a trend line or as a separate, more horizontal line. Strong resistance is where the moving line goes up and touches the resistance line several times, only to retreat. When a breakout occurs through resistance, it is a sign of strength in the stock market. In the bond market, when resistance is broken through, it's a sign of bond sellers. When resistance is penetrated, it will often convert to being support.

Trends, support, and resistance are basic analytical forms of technical analysis. They tend to be followed by many fundamental analysts as well. The belief is that trends show the current direction and to some extent strength of the current market.

PATTERNS

Many technical analysts follow chart patterns, the different shapes made by a trend over time. Such patterns as head and shoulders, symmetrical triangle, ascending right triangle, descending right triangle, rectangle, pennant, flag, and even the cup and handle are some of the many chart patterns that many believe have predictive qualities. For example, a pattern where the moving line forms the shape of a head and shoulders is thought to predict a drop. It also has a measure for the drop. Once the breakout occurs to the downside, the drop will be at least the same as the distance from the top of the head to the neckline. That's a minimum; it could be more.

Does it work? A qualified yes is the definitive answer. Yes, many times a drop appears after a head and shoulders pattern, but not always. When it doesn't appear, the pattern becomes referred to as a simple consolidation. Even with the great amount of subjectivity in technical analysis, many use it for stock and bond trading, both at the professional and individual levels. The complete study of patterns is a subject covered elsewhere. Here, we are more concerned with understanding simple trend lines, support, and resistance.

NEED TO KNOW

For individual investment portfolios, the need-to-know information is what will provide a general understanding of things that affect the economy. Learning about trend lines and what is meant by support and resistance can be important. Such knowledge can help the investor understand more about the strength and direction of the markets. If someone has the intellect and the interest, each area of analysis can be explored to great depths, but the real effect that understanding will have on an individual's portfolio is likely to be modest. Investment gains tend to be made by individuals when they do enough analysis to understand what might happen and then have the nerve and the assets to follow a strategy.

CHAPTER 31

Check Out the DANs

New investment products seem to appear every year. Many new products are designed for institutional investors and traders, but occasionally a new one appears for the individual investor. Direct access notes (or DANs) are a straightforward fixed-income security designed to allow individuals to buy corporate bonds direct from major U.S. corporations as original issue securities.

CONVENIENCE

DANs are designed for the individual investor. They offer unique features to simplify and streamline the investment process. DANs are sold directly to the individual investor usually at par (or face value amount, typically $1000 per note). DANs trade and settle flat, meaning they have no accrued interest, on a regular way basis, which requires payment by the third business day following the purchase. The investor knows the coupon and yield prior to purchase.

TIME TO EVALUATE

Direct access notes are designed for individuals who make their investment decisions with time and reflection. DANs are announced on a Friday and are usually available until the following Thursday. The time gives investors a chance to weigh the value of the investment. This can be a big advantage over buying regular corporate bonds, where a firm price quotation is only good for a few minutes.

WEEKLY NEW DANs

New DANs are announced periodically, generally weekly, with the information available through a retail representative or at the DAN website: *direct-notes.com*.

FLEXIBILITY

Every investor has individual investment objectives and needs. DANs offer a variety of alternatives to enable each investor to enhance portfolio structures with strategies. DANs offer the fixed-income investor a selection of maturities to match time requirements. Cash flows are also important for a fixed-income investor. Payment options include monthly and six-month payment dates. Both callable and noncallable notes are available.

YIELDS

The return on any investment should be in proportion to the risk. Bonds with longer maturities have higher returns. Bonds issued by firms with higher business risk will offer higher yields. Direct access notes can likely offer a bond or a combination of bonds to fit the needs of many investors' portfolios.

MAJOR CORPORATE NAMES

Investing in large, well-known companies can have advantages. Investors are likely to be familiar with products marketed by the issuers. All issuers are large U.S. corporations who file all the standard SEC documents. Copies of these documents are available from the issuer or from other sources. Direct access notes are sold by prospectus, which gives an overview of the issuer and detailed information on the notes.

SURVIVOR'S OPTION

DANs are issued with a *survivor's option*, which allows the estate of the bondholder to return the bond to the company at par (100% of the purchase price) in the event of the bondholder's death. In effect, this feature is a put that says investors aren't transferring bond-pricing risk to their estates. The feature thereby enables investors to match investments with estate planning.

GMAC DANs

An example of a direct access note comes from the General Motors Acceptance Corporation (GMAC). The following gives some details. The information presented here is for illustrative purposes only and should not be considered a recommendation to buy or sell securities.

General Motors Acceptance Corporation SmartNotes
Senior Unsecured Medium-Term Notes
Offered for: January 22, 1999, to January 28, 1999

Coupon	Payment	Maturity	Callable	Survivor's Option	Price[1]	Yield[2]	APY[3]
5.125%	Monthly**	2/15/02	NC	Yes	100	5.180%	5.147%
5.350%	Semi-An	2/15/04	NC	Yes	100	5.350%	5.422%
5.500%	Monthly	2/15/09	NC	Yes	100	5.563%	5.641%
6.250%	Monthly	2/15/14	NC 3*	Yes	100	6.332%	6.432%

* This issue is callable at par as of 2/15/02, and every remaining coupon date.
** All monthly payments are made on the fifteenth of the month.
1 The prices are quoted as a percentage of par.
2 Yields are quoted on a semi-annual bond equivalent yield basis.
3 Annual percentage yield.

DANs MIGHT BE USEFUL

Direct access notes offer convenient, flexible access to major corporate names and can be a useful investment, depending on objectives, in an individual's diversified portfolio.[1] Although many individuals like the feature of a monthly payment, a payment every six months can be placed in an interest-bearing account for nearly the same effect. Interested investors should obtain and read a copy of the prospectus available.

---

1 Based on information from ABN AMRO Incorporated, 208 S. LaSalle St., Chicago, IL 60604, 1998–1999, http://www.direct-notes.com/.

CHAPTER 32

Don't Fight the Fed

What exactly is "the Fed?" It is the Federal Reserve Bank, the central bank of the United States. Established in 1913, it was—and is—charged with fostering a sound banking system and healthy economy. The Fed is a bankers' bank as well as the bank for the federal government. It also serves as a regulator of financial institutions as well as the nation's money manager, performing several functions that affect the economy, financial system, and individuals.

MONEY MANAGER

The most important of the Fed's responsibilities is formulating and carrying out monetary policy, i.e., acting as the nation's "money manager." It strives to balance the flow of money and credit with the needs of the economy. Too much money in the economy can lead to inflation, while too little slows growth. The Fed tries to strike a balance between the two extremes and foster economic growth with price stability.

To achieve this balance, the Fed works to control money at its source by influencing the ability of financial institutions to "create" checkbook money through loans or investments. The leverage that the Fed uses in this process is the "reserves" that banks and thrifts must maintain.

CASH RESERVE REQUIREMENTS

Depository institutions are subject to rules that require a certain percentage of deposits to be set aside as reserves and not used for loans or investments. Institutions meet these requirements with cash in their own vaults and balances in a reserve account at a Fed bank. The reserve balances and requirements determine how much money an institution can create through lending and investing. Through reserves, the Fed indirectly affects the flow of money and credit through the economy.

THREE TOOLS FOR AFFECTING RESERVES

Reserve Requirements

The Fed can alter the percentage of deposits that institutions must set aside as reserves. Lowering reserve requirements tends to inject money into the economy by releasing funds that were previously set aside. Increasing the requirements ties up funds that financial institutions could otherwise pump into the economy. The Fed seldom changes reserve requirements because of the dramatic effect that it can have on institutions and the economy.

Discount Rate

An increase in the discount rate tends to inhibit the lending and investment activity of financial institutions. However, if money is readily available from sources other than the Fed's "discount window," a discount rate change won't have as much impact. A change in the discount rate can also be a signal of the Fed's policy direction. Obviously, if the Fed is increasing the discount rate, it is tightening money. If the rate is lowered, the Fed is assuming a loosening posture.

Open Market Operations

The most flexible, therefore important, monetary policy tools are open market operations. They are the purchase and sale of government securities by the Fed. When the Fed wants to increase the flow of money and credit, it buys government securities, putting cash into the economy. When it wants to restrict the flow of money and credit, it sells government securities, thereby removing cash from the economy.

FEDERAL DISCOUNT RATE

One way the Fed maintains a sound banking system is as "lender of last resort." A financial institution experiencing a drain on deposits can turn to its Reserve Bank if unable to borrow money elsewhere. A loan from the Fed enables an institution to get through temporary difficulties and helps prevent difficulties at one financial institution from spreading to others. The interest rate charged for these loans is called the federal discount rate (Figure 32–1).

FIGURE 32–1

Federal Discount Rate, 1958–1998

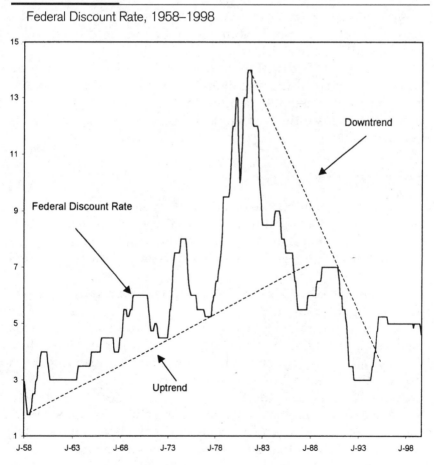

Although the federal discount rate is changed periodically, there is no limit to how many times it can be changed in a given year. There were several changes between 1990 and 1992 (Figure 32–1). At this point, money was being made available to stimulate the economy. The most dramatic tightening of money occurred in the 1977–1981 period, when inflation was in an upward spiral of wage and price increases.

DON'T FIGHT THE FED WITH BONDS

In a perfect world of investing, a bond investor would have bought 2-year or 3-year bonds with interest rates in an uptrend (1956–1981). As interest rates turned, the 10-year, 20-year, or 30-year bonds would have been obtained on the way down. But it's not a perfect world, and future events are difficult to forecast. The interest rate peaks in 1960, 1969, and 1974 undoubtedly produced bond yields that were difficult to resist.

Fighting the Fed with bonds would be to lock in long-term yields as rates are rising and likely to continue upward. As rates turn and decline steadily, fighting the Fed would be to reinvest short-term yields rather than to lock in something higher for the long-term.

DON'T GET FAKED OUT

As discussed earlier, the federal discount rate is the amount of interest charged by the Fed when financial institutions need to borrow cash to meet minimum reserve requirements. The institutions can also borrow from each other. The rate charged them is referred to as "fed funds."

Although fed-funds is more of an interbank rate, it can be influenced by the Federal Reserve. At times, the Fed will influence the fed funds rate rather than change the discount rate. Remember, the reasoning behind the Fed's actions is to either slow the economy by raising rates or stimulate the economy by lowering rates. Slowing the economy also means stopping inflation.

In March of 1997, the Fed exerted its influence on the fed-funds rate by raising it a quarter of a percent to 5.5%. To some investors, this represented an ominous signal of higher interest rates. To others, it showed that the Fed was serious about acting swiftly

FIGURE 32–2

S&P 500 Index and 30-Year Treasury Yields 1996–1998

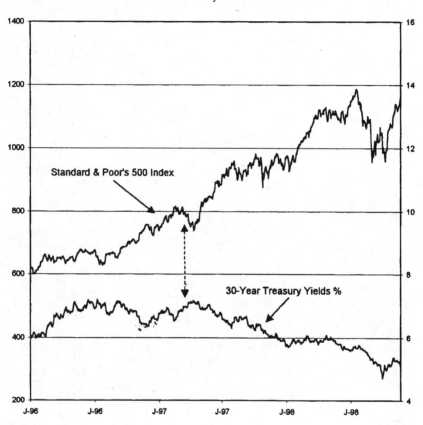

to prevent inflation. The "others" reasoned that interest rates should be coming down due to the overall economic situation and that this was a short-term rise.

They were correct. One increase of either the federal discount rate or the fed-funds rate does not necessarily mean interest rates will continue to rise (see Figure 32–2). It's usually better to follow the trend and economic commentaries rather than isolated incidents.

CHAPTER 33

Watch the
Stock Market

Ever since Charles Henry Dow published his first Dow Industrial Average, investors have looked to the stock market for an indication of the direction and strength of the market and therefore of the economy. Many believe the stock market to be the topside of the economy, with the consumer or end user being the bottom. Purchases of consumers and other end users put cash earnings on the bottom line of the company that made the product. Since investors in the stock market anticipate and attempt to be efficient, those purchases affecting earnings also become a factor in whether a company's stock will be bought or sold.

ANTICIPATION

A person can correctly analyze the stock market, but it doesn't do much good if one waits to see if the conclusions are accurate and then buys at the top or sells at the bottom. In some ways, bonds have an advantage. An investor wouldn't buy because of a belief that interest rates will rise. The investor can wait to see if the analysis assumptions are correct.

Investing requires a certain amount of anticipation, looking ahead and drawing conclusions as to what might happen next. Anticipation can be easily interrupted by unexpected realities. The stock market can take a sudden nosedive and drop 300 points or more.

Interest rates can suddenly move up a notch because of influence from the Federal Reserve Bank. Most sudden, unexpected moves are short-lived and shouldn't stop the investor from anticipation.

INDICATORS

Anticipation relies on indicators. It must always be remembered that indicators are not predictors. If a car is driving down the street and has its left turn signal on, does it mean the driver will turn left? No, it's only an indicator of what is likely to happen. Stock and bond market indicators are similar in nature. They indicate; they do not predict.

THE STOCK MARKET AS INDICATOR

If the stock market reflects the general health of the economy and that is related to yields on bonds, then it's only logical that the stock market can be an indicator for bonds. If we look at market history, some evidence appears. Figure 33–1 looks at the daily closing levels of the Standard & Poor's 500 Index in comparison to 30-year Treasury bond yields in the period from 1989 to 1991.

A strong stock market in 1989 got even stronger as interest rates moved lower, dropping a total of 1.41% from the highest to the lowest point. It appeared clear that the Federal Reserve had a stimulating posture toward the economy. Interest rates were down and looked like they might go lower. On October 13, the stock market got a case of the October blues and the Standard & Poor's 500 Index dropped 21.74 points (6.5%). The Dow Industrial Average dropped 190.58 points, not a record but definitely a significant correction.

WHAT HAPPENED TO YIELDS?

Look at what happened to the yields. Rather, look at what didn't happen. A hint of an increase can be seen, but it wasn't significant. Although at the time there were fears that this October correction would be a replay of the severe correction in 1987, it didn't happen. Bond traders and mutual fund holders held tight, believing this to be just a short-term correction. They were right and the market continued upward, in spite of growing troubles in the Middle East.

FIGURE 33-1

FIGURE 33-1

Market as Indicator, S&P 500 Index and 30-Year, 1989–1991

TROUBLE WITH OIL

The trouble with oil is that we need so much of it, and it's a limited resource. It is essential to commerce; therefore it is essential to economic stability and growth. When oil is threatened or restricted, it can send the economy and the markets into turmoil.

That was precisely the situation in mid-1990. The heated conflict in the Persian Gulf brought uncertainty to the economy, the stock market, and the bond market. Stock prices plummeted, sending the S&P 500 Index 24% lower in a big hurry. The index dropped 68.96 points between July and October.

The stock market turned first, but bonds were right behind. Yields on the long bond were at about 8.5%, but they quickly broke through 9%. Of course, the conflict was short-lived and so were the high interest rates. The stance of the Fed remained accommodating, and yields on the long bond came back down to 8.5% and lower.

WHAT ABOUT RECENTLY?

It's been more of the same, at least for a while. Long bond yields have remained low and moved even lower. Yields moved up a percent in early 1996 and remained just above 7% until April of 1997, when they again moved lower. In October of 1998, yields were at 4.75% on the 30-year Treasury bond (Figure 33–2). From this point

F I G U R E 33–2

Market as Indicator, S&P 500 Index and 30-Year, 1996–1998

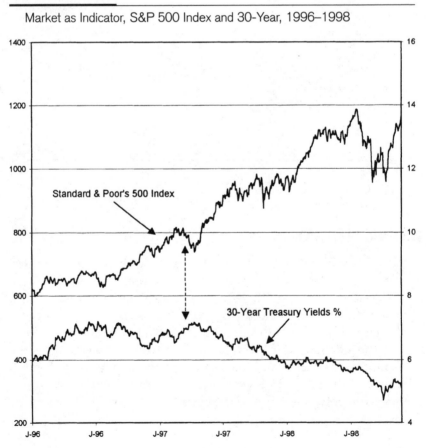

to the end of 1998, we see the yields move steadily lower as the stock market goes essentially flat or up.

Market corrections appear in these three years, but the interest rate increases are minor and don't last long. A sharp correction in October of 1997 dropped the S&P Index more than 91 points. In the same correction, the Dow Industrials set a new record for a one-day loss, down 554.26 points. But it was a bit of a yawn. The markets recovered quickly and business moved on to the next crisis.

The next economic threat came from Asia. Markets started getting nervous toward the end of July 1998 and dropped until the end of August. The S&P Index dropped 226.82 points (24.6%), and the Dow Industrial Average went down 1756.68 points (23.3%), creating another of those short bear markets.[1]

But look at the bond yields in 1998. They barely moved. Interest rates were kept down even though the stock market was in a bearish mood.

NOT THE ONLY INDICATOR

The most successful investors watch more than one indicator to provide signals of changes in interest rates. Whereas the stock market is an indicator of strength in the economy, short-term weaknesses can be misleading. The sharp market corrections with short duration seem to appear more frequently when interest rates are low and the market is high.

---

1 The term *bear market* doesn't have a set definition. The Dow Industrial Average being down more than 20% or down for more than two consecutive months is accepted by many as being a bear market.

CHAPTER 34

Look for a Flight to Quality

An evening news report might start with a headline like this:

> Stocks ended lower today as Brazil announced a currency devaluation. The Dow Industrial Average dropped more than 200 points by noon and closed down 260 points for the day. In a suspected flight to quality, bonds rallied early in the morning and stayed strong throughout the day, as did the Dow Utility Average.

NERVOUS MARKET

Occasionally, the financial markets get nervous. They show unexpected volatility during a time of relative stability. A number of investors, professional and individual, sell securities at risk (usually common stock) and buy securities with a perceived lower risk. Many times, the lower-risk securities will be bonds and utility common stock. The activities of these investors in flight cause bond prices and utility common stock prices to rise. The activity is frequently referred to as a *flight to quality*. The price increases are usually temporary and settle back to a previous pattern in a few days.

NOT TIME TO BUY BONDS

Obviously, if a flight to quality is occurring, it is not the ideal time to be buying bonds. Prices go up and yields go down. Although it's not a good time to buy bonds, it might be a good time to sell bonds and take advantage of the price blip.

A NOTE OF CAUTION

Although the flight to quality is like the fabled boy who cried "wolf," it is conceivable that a time could arise when a flight to quality is justified, for example, when a long-term serious economic problem suddenly appears. Keeping informed and updated on news developments can help the investor be aware of economic difficulties. An investment decision can be made based on the information gathered.

Buy "Junk" Bonds for Higher Yield

A "high yield," or "junk," bond is issued by a company considered to have higher credit risk than for rated bonds. High-yield bonds are considered to be speculative, i.e., below investment grade. They have either a lower rating or no rating from the bond rating agencies.

SALES PITCH

It's important to understand that a junk bond company's credit might be acceptable, they just decided to issue nonrated bonds, which would be more easily marketed. At least, that was the sales pitch during the golden age of junk bonds in the 1980s.

The chance of default with junk bonds is greater than for bonds with investment grade credit ratings (BBB or better). Higher risk, in this situation, means higher yields than bonds with better bond ratings.

IMPORTANT REALIZATION

The so called junk bond debacle of the 1980s brought an important realization to investors. Not all junk bonds default. In fact, most do not. The issuing companies continue to pay the high rate of interest until maturity or call the bonds and refinance with rated bonds.

RATING SYSTEM

Junk bonds get their name from the way credit ratings were developed for bonds. Rating agencies created a grading system to summarize the credit quality of issuers. The highest-grade bonds are AAA, with the scale descending to C. Defaulted bonds are labeled D, which is a fact and not really a rating. Bonds with an acceptable risk of default are BBB bonds and higher, collectively referred to as *investment grade*. Bonds rated BB or lower are *speculative grade* and obviously have a higher risk of default.

HISTORY OF THE NAME

Bond ratings eventually became the basis of investment policies for financial institutions. Government regulatory bodies also accepted bond rating standards for the establishment of investing policies. With most professional investors being restricted by investment policy, investment grade and higher bonds were widely held, but speculative bonds were not. Few mainstream dealers carried the bonds, and eventually they came to be called junk bonds.

JUNK BONDS BECOME PRODUCT

Before junk bonds became so popular in the late 1980s, they were usually rated bonds whose credit rating had been lowered. The nickname for them had been "fallen angels." In the 1980s, portfolio managers began to look at *risk-adjusted* returns for junk bonds and found them high, meaning risk was compensated by higher yields.

Later, brokerage firm Drexel-Burnham and Michael Millken led a large investment foray into junk bonds. Unfortunately, this ended with a scandal and the collapse of several junk bond issuers. Several of these issuers recovered in the 1990s and they are currently thriving at the end of the decade. In the 1990s, several mutual funds have formed portfolios containing junk bonds exclusively.

BOND FUNDS

As discussed in Chapter 9, bond mutual funds have considerable market risk because with the open-ended fund there is no way to hold a bond to maturity. However, with high-risk junk bonds, although the no-maturity risk still exists, a fund will add diversification and some protection against individual issue defaults. If the yield spread is large enough, the fund might be the best way to go. However, such an investment should be with speculative money.

MARKET LIQUIDITY

Lack of liquidity is one of the risks of high-yield investing and is another reason junk bonds pay higher yields. Liquidity, defined as trading bonds without initiating major changes in prices, varies with both general market conditions and the size and type of bond. Large, well-known companies often enjoy greater liquidity for their bonds than smaller companies do. Less liquidity makes higher transaction costs. Lower liquidity can also cause greater price volatility.

NARROWED SPREAD

The average yield spread over the past 10 years has been 5.6%, but the high part of that average occurred a few years back. In early 1990, the average yield of junk was 17%, but in early 1999, it has shrunk to about 8.5%. Although that might be a high yield in fixed-income investing, it's not much better than highly rated bonds. It might be acceptable to professional portfolio managers, but they take more losses than individuals can afford.[1]

YIELD SPREAD

Anytime an investor decides to speculate for higher yields by buying lower-rated or nonrated bonds, the yield spread should be checked. Another decision is how much of a spread over safer, rated bonds compensates for the additional risk. The real question is whether a yield spread of 3%, junk over Treasuries, is enough to justify the higher risk. It might be acceptable to some investors, but many times a lower-rated investment grade bond will be a more prudent selection.

---

1 "Are Junk Bonds in Your Future?" Consumer Affairs Department of The Institute of Certified Financial Planners, provided courtesy of The Los Angeles Society of the Institute of Certified Financial Planners, November 30, 1997, http://www.laicfp.org/jbonds.html.

CHAPTER 36

Do "Swaps" for Money Now

Swap: to trade one thing for another. With bonds swapping is usually done to create a tax loss. The investor sells bonds after interest rates have risen and pushed the bond prices lower. The bonds in an investment portfolio are sold and other bonds are purchased. The end result is a new set of bonds and a tax loss. The swap converted the "paper loss" to a real loss, which can be used to offset other capital gains and up to $3000 of ordinary income.

LOOK OUT FOR THE WASH SALE

If a taxpayer sells an ailing security to create a loss, that investor cannot buy the same or what the IRS considers a "substantially identical" security within 30 days of the sale. Losses from such so-called "wash sales" are not deductible.

Bond swaps can help reduce taxes without the 30-day wait as long as investors buy slightly different bonds. Bond swaps work better than other securities swaps because it's easier to find other bonds with significantly different characteristics, such as yields, issuers, and maturity dates. The investor still ends up with a comparable investment and doesn't lose the tax advantage. Tax-loss selling isn't the only reason to do a swap, however.

INTEREST RATES RISING

If interest rates have shown some increase and the prevailing belief is that they will go even higher, it could make sense to swap out of long-term bonds into something shorter. The swap will reduce market risk. The short-term bond prices have less fluctuation but can also make cash available sooner if the interest rates do indeed continue to move upward.

INTEREST RATES DECLINING

When interest rates are likely to go lower, an *extension swap* might be useful to the investor. This entails selling some short-term securities and buying long-term before the rates go lower. Of course, this strategy would depend on the yields of bonds currently in the portfolio. It would only be worthwhile if the end result provided some improvement.

QUALITY SWAP

If the yield spreads have narrowed, it might make sense to swap to bonds of a higher quality. When the yield differences between high-quality and low-quality bonds are minimal, sell the low-quality and buy the higher-rated bonds. It can lower risk on the portfolio with minimal yield sacrifice.

Looking the other direction, if analysis shows the credit situation of a company is improving and it no longer deserves its low bond rating, a worthwhile strategy might be for an investor to buy a lower-quality, higher-yield bond. The strategy does require analysis into the financial structure of the company and its bonds.

CALL EXTENSION

If bonds are approaching a call date, you can swap them for bonds with a call date farther in the future. Beat the issuer to the call and do it when the advantage is on your side. We all know the present, but none of us truly knows the future. If callable bonds are likely to be called in the next year or less, make the swap now, when the information available can be of use.

TAXABLE FOR TAX-FREE

Depending on the individual situation, it might become more profitable for an investor to increase the tax-exempt or municipal bond portion of the portfolio. The double and triple tax-exempt bonds can allow the investor to keep more money by not spending so much on taxes. Refer to Chapter 37 for more on taxable equivalent yield, a formula for determining whether the municipal bond or the corporate bond has a higher yield when taxes are considered.

TO SWAP OR HOLD

The decision to swap or hold takes some analysis of the current bond position, financial situation of the investor, and the characteristics or advantages of the new bond purchase. When swaps are done, it should be with a thorough understanding of what is to be accomplished. Is the swap for a deduction on capital gains or income, or is it being done to improve the quality of the portfolio?

CHAPTER 37

You Don't Have to Pay Taxes on Bonds

Tax-exempt municipal bonds are debt obligations issued by municipalities, states, cities, counties, and other governmental entities. The borrowing is to raise money for building schools, highways, hospitals, and sewer systems, as well as many other projects for the public good. While there are several types of investments that provide an investor with tax-exempt income, they all utilize municipal bonds as their source.

The purchase of a municipal bond lends money to an issuer who promises to pay a specified amount of interest (usually paid semiannually) and return the principal on a specified date (maturity).

NO TAX

Interest income on most municipal bonds is exempt from federal and in some cases, state and local income taxes for those living in the state of issue. Being tax-exempt enables local and state governments to borrow money at lower interest costs than corporations or even the federal government. The lower cost of borrowing obviously saves these entities money. The tax-exempt status also makes the bonds highly attractive to investors.[1]

---

1 For some tax-exempt municipal bonds, some investors' income may be subject to the Federal Alternative Minimum Tax.

TAXABLE EQUIVALENT YIELD

One way to look at tax-free bonds and non-tax-free bonds is to calculate the *taxable equivalent yield*. The taxable equivalent yield is the interest a non-tax-free bond would have to pay to equal the return on a tax-free bond. Anything larger indicates the non-tax-free bond is a better deal. A lesser amount indicates the tax-free bond is better.

Taxable equivalent yield = Tax-free yield (stated as a decimal) ÷ 1.00 – the investor's tax bracket (stated as a decimal)

For example, assume that the investor is considering a 6% municipal bond and that the investor is in the 28% tax bracket.

$$6\% \div 100 = 0.06$$
$$28\% \div 100 = 0.28$$
$$1.00 - 0.28 = 0.72$$
$$0.06 \div 0.72 = 0.0833, \text{ or } 8.33\%$$

A taxable bond would have to pay an investor in the 28% tax bracket 8.33% to equal the return on a tax-free bond. Anything higher than 8.33% on a taxable corporate would make it the higher-yielding bond.

UNDERSTANDING YIELDS

Like other types of bonds, munis have current yields and yield to maturity. Current yield is the annual return on the dollar amount paid for a bond (essentially, coupon dollar amount divided by current price).

Yield to maturity is the return received by holding a bond until it matures. The calculation includes price, coupon, and time as factors. It can provide a quick comparison of one bond to another.

When the price of a tax-exempt bond increases above its face value, it is said to be selling at a premium. When the bond sells below face value, it is selling at a discount. Price changes with bonds are determined by changes in interest rates.

MUNIS HAVE BOND RATINGS

Munis also have credit ratings. Many are graded by agencies such as Moody's Investors Service, Standard & Poor's Corporation, and

Fitch Investors Service, Inc. In addition, some banks and brokerage firms have research departments to analyze muni bonds.

Bond credit ratings are important, they reflect a professional assessment of the issuer's ability to pay interest and return the bond's face value at maturity. Bonds rated BBB, BAA, or better by Standard & Poor's, Fitch, or Moody's, respectively, are generally considered investment grade, suitable for preservation of investment capital. Obviously, more risk-aversive investors can raise that to say AA or better and speculative investors can lower the standard for higher yields.

MARKET RISK

While the coupon rate cannot be changed during the existence of a bond (except for a variable-rate security), the market price changes as market conditions change. If munis are sold before reaching maturity, they receive the current market price. If the bonds were purchased at face value (par) and interest rates have risen, selling will bring less than face value. If interest rates are lower, the price will be higher than face value.

MUNI CALLS

Many bonds allow the issuer to call all or part of the issue at a premium, or at face value, before they reach maturity. When buying muni bonds, the investor should ask about call provisions.

SPECIAL FEATURES

Insured Municipal Bonds

Some municipal bond issues are insured to reduce investment risk. If the bonds default, the insurance company guarantees payment of both interest and principal when due. The cost for the insurance comes out of the yield. In other words, insured bonds normally have lower yields than comparable uninsured bonds.

Floating Rate and Variable Rate Bonds

Here, the interest payment from the bond changes as interest rates change. The rate is generally based on U.S. Treasury yields or on some other basic index.

Zero-Coupon Muni Bonds

Like other zeroes, munis are issued at a deep discount from their face value at maturity. They do not pay out interest. Instead, it compounds at the stated interest rate. The investor receives one payment containing principal and interest at maturity. Zeroes are especially well-suited for investors who do not need the current cash flow from investments.

Put Bonds

A put feature on some munis allows the bondholder to turn in the bond at face value on a specified date before the maturity date. The feature makes the bonds more attractive to those who believe interest rates might go higher. The bonds can be put and the principal reinvested at higher yields.

TYPES OF MUNICIPAL BONDS

Municipal securities have short- and long-term issues. Short-term, often called notes, usually mature in a year or less. Short-term notes are used to raise money in anticipation of future revenues. The money might be needed to meet unanticipated deficits or raise cash for projects temporarily until longer bond financing can be arranged. Anticipated revenues could be taxes, state or federal aid payments, or bond proceeds. Short-term notes pay interest on maturity. Long-term bonds normally have maturities of more than a year (2 to 30 years). Bonds are usually sold to finance capital projects over the longer term. They normally pay interest every six months. The basic types of municipal securities are as follows.

General Obligation Bonds (GO Bonds)

The payment of principal and interest are secured by the full faith and credit of the issuer. General obligation bonds are by the issuer's ability to tax.

Revenue Bonds (Rev Bonds)

The payment of principal and interest is secured by the revenues earned by the facility that was constructed using the money from the bond issue. Public-use projects like highways, bridges, airports, commercial boat landings, water and sewage treatment facilities, hospitals, and housing for the poor are constructed with the funds from municipal revenue bonds. Revenue bonds normally do not depend on the taxing ability of a municipality; therefore, they can have some higher risk in certain situations. The revenue-generating facility has to earn enough income to meet the interest and principal payments.

Minimum Investment

Most tax-exempt municipal bonds are issued in denominations of $5000 or integral multiples of $5000. Most notes are also available in a minimum denomination of $5000. Bond mutual funds and unit trusts can have different minimum requirements.

Marketability

Holders of municipal securities can sell their notes or bonds in the secondary market through one of the more than 2000 banks and securities dealers that are registered to buy and sell municipal securities. Municipal bonds are sold in the over-the-counter market instead of on an organized exchange. If an investor sells bonds prior to maturity and receives the current market price, it might be more or less than the original cost.

Costs of Municipal Bonds

Municipal securities are bought and sold between dealers and investors much like other bonds and debt securities. Dealers trade the securities at a net cost. In other words, the cost is stated as a part of the bond price.

Gains and Losses

If tax-exempt securities are sold before maturity and are sold at a gain, the gain is fully taxable. Only the interest received is tax-exempt, not any capital gains from selling early.

If the securities are sold for less than the original purchase price, there will obviously be a capital loss. Part of the loss might be deductible from the investor's ordinary earned income.

Special rules apply to tax-exempt bonds purchased at a premium or a discount and called or sold before maturity. A tax accountant should be consulted in these matters, since tax laws are subject to change.

READY? CHECK THE YIELD CURVE

When the investor is ready to buy munis, or any bond, the first thing to check is the current yield curve. The yield curve for munis can be based on national munis (federal tax-exempt but not state), or it can be on local bond issues (talk to a banker or broker). The main thing to look for on the yield curve is the consistent yield spread as the maturity dates get longer. Is the 10-year muni yielding more than the 5-year? Less than the 20-year bond?

The national muni yield curve for January 21, 1999 (Figure 37–1), shows a good 1.75% spread between the 2-year and 30-year municipal bonds. The curve appears to be normal, meaning each farther maturity has a higher yield. The munis are paying higher yields for the investor to accept longer-term risk.

If the yield curve is satisfactory, it's time to check the availability of desirable local munis. Availability from state to state can vary dramatically, but all one has to do is call a bank representative or a broker and ask what yields are available on local munis.

Determine the spread between local (state and federal tax-exempt) muni yields and corporate bonds or Treasury bonds. Calculate the taxable equivalent yield (formula earlier in this chapter) and decide whether the tax-exempt muni is the best selection. Perhaps corporate bonds or Treasury bonds will bring in more money. Once the yields are compared, the length of maturity is decided on. All that remains is to place the order based on availability.

NATIONAL AND OTHER STATE MUNIS

Mutual funds and unit trusts will often do national muni groupings. These might consist of several issues from several states. The bonds are often selected for high yield, but they are only federal tax-exempt. In order for a muni to maintain its tax-exempt status from state and local government, it must be a muni from the investor's state of primary residence, where the investor pays income tax.

F I G U R E   37–1

Yield Curve, National Municipal Bonds, January 21, 1999

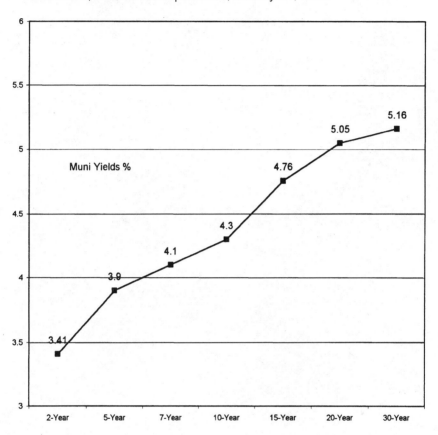

PART OF A PORTFOLIO

Tax-exempt municipal bonds can be an important part of an investor's portfolio. Obviously, the tax-exemption is a large benefit to many, but muni bonds are also important to the community. It's a way of investing in one's home state. The funds for the bonds often do much to improve the quality of life for everyone living in the state.

Bonds Are Safe If Held to Maturity

Bonds, whether corporate or the highly regarded U.S. Treasury bonds, are safe if the investor holds them to maturity. Investors and traders deal in a risk-oriented business. The entire money world is about taking risk for a return.

PRICE RISK FIRST

The first and most common perception of risk is price. Too many people don't go any farther than price. Although change in price is the first, most dramatic manifestation of risk, there are many other factors. A change in price might only be a symptom to consider in making an investment decision.

RISK MANAGEMENT

One thing about risk: Although it cannot be eliminated, it can be managed so it has minimal impact on the financial future of the investor. In order to manage risk, it has to be defined more precisely than the possibility of a change in price. Moreover, when one risk is eliminated, another usually appears. It is not possible to eliminate all risk from an investment action.

CREDIT RISK

As discussed in Chapter 5, a higher yield can be had by investing in lower-quality issues. Usually, the lower the quality, the higher the yield. The higher yield on lower-quality bond issues supposedly makes up for the higher risk of nonpayment (default).

Obviously, it is only income if the bond issuer pays when due and returns the face value at the call or at maturity. Junk bonds and low-rated bonds have super-high yields for a good reason. The bondholder might not be paid either the interest or principal. Avoiding credit risk involves the other extreme. If only the very highest-quality bond issues are selected, the yield might be low, lower than other, reasonably secure bonds. If the yield difference is wide enough, the risk of loss by default is replaced by the certainty of a lower yield.

The "spread" between yields of different quality securities constantly changes. Each time an investment decision is made, the yield spread should be examined to choose the most desirable trade-off between credit risk and income.

There are times when the difference between the yield of the highest-quality issues (Treasury bills, notes, and bonds) and other issues is so minor that there is no point in accepting a bond of lower quality. It doesn't make much sense to buy a yield from a corporate issuer that is only a half a percent better than a Treasury issue of comparable maturity.

INTEREST RATE AND MATURITY RISK

Longer bond maturities have greater price fluctuations than short-term bonds. The longer the maturity, the more volatile the price with any change in yields. Also, there is a tendency for lower-coupon-rate (the stated interest rate of the bond) bonds to be more volatile when they are long-term. If an investor anticipates needing some of the cash before a long-term bond would mature, an estimate of the amount should be invested short-term.

Buying short-term reduces the price risk inherent in the longer maturity, but it also makes a larger current investment necessary. And it sacrifices stable income because the money is reinvested at constantly changing short-term rates. The only gain for the sacrifice is strength of principal, when the money is returned at the short-term maturity dates.

Longer maturities usually provide higher yields. The "shape" of the yield curve changes continually. At times, there is only a small difference between the yield on the 10-year and 30-year bonds. During these times, it doesn't make sense to have the greater price risk of the long bond for only a small increase in yield. Other times, the longer-bond yields are high enough to justify the increased price risk.

The yield curve can reveal potential risk when it is inverted. If short-term yields become higher than long-term, the yield curve is signaling an expected decrease in future interest rates. As shown in Chapter 4, the drop might be preceded by sharp and sudden increases.

When the yield curve is steep and positive, yielding much more in the long bonds than in the short bonds, the curve is often forecasting rising rates in the future. Recessions are frequently preceded by an inverted or a flat yield curve.

INCOME AND REINVESTMENT RISK

If an income investor buys long bonds for the yield, it is locked in no matter what happens to future interest rates. There is income risk in the sense of inflation, meaning rising prices. The investor's cost of living could go up and the income from the bond might become inadequate. Furthermore, higher rates will make the value of the bonds decline, creating a loss of capital if it becomes necessary to sell some of them. That risk can be considerable, especially with long-term bonds.

In a period of declining rates, the investor receives the benefits of constant income and theoretically lower cost-of-living prices while the value of the bonds increases. The investor isn't able to take advantage of the increased value (unless the bonds are used as collateral) because if sold, the investor could not replace the income and keep the same quality and maturity.

BOND ARE SAFE IF HELD TO MATURITY

That statement refers only to market price risk. No matter what happens to the market price of the bond, if the issuer is able to make interest and principal payments, the face value (par value) will be returned at maturity.

CHAPTER 39

Know the Bond Rating

Bond credit ratings give an important insight into the risk of investing. Higher ratings tend to pay lower interest rates, and lower ratings pay greater amounts of interest. An investor can choose to accept more risk for higher reward or be conservative with a lower, safer return on investment. Some bonds are (N/R), meaning not rated. They tend to pay the highest rates of interest and have the greatest amount of risk. Because of the risk involved, nonrated bonds are usually referred to as junk bonds.

WHY RATE BONDS?

When an investor puts money on the line, it's nice to have some reassurance that the money will be paid back. When banks lend money to individuals, they gather information that could have a bearing on the borrower's ability to repay. It's their way of managing risk. Rather than examining the creditworthiness of several companies, an individual can manage risk by investing in bonds that have higher ratings. The rating agencies have already done the analysis.

U.S. Treasury bills, notes, and bonds always have the highest rating of AAA. When purchased and held to maturity, they are considered to be the safest investments in the world. (Caution: If treasury investments are bought and sold, the risk increases dramatically due to possible interest rate and consequent price changes.)

WHAT IS A BOND RATING?

Although bonds are generally considered safer, more conservative investments than common stock, they still depend on an issuer's ability to pay the interest and return the principal at maturity. All of this is essentially based on the issuing authority's creditworthiness. Rather than take on the enormous task of determining each company's ability to pay interest and return principal, investors tend to rely on rating agencies to classify the credit risk of bonds. The ratings represent a considerable amount of research and analysis.

Ratings are stated in an abbreviated letter system, with the triple A (AAA or Aaa) being the best. The rating does not guarantee the safety of the bonds or interest payments; it merely states that the issuer should be able to meet the debt servicing obligation by making the scheduled interest payments and the return of face value. In other words, a rating is an opinion based on research and analysis of a financial condition. If an issuer of a bond cannot make one of the interest payments, it is referred to as "being in default."

WHOOPS

When two partially completed projects were canceled, the Washington Public Power Supply System (WPPSS), a consortium of utilities building nuclear power plants in the Pacific Northwest, went bankrupt. The $2.25 billion in default bonds (first in 1982) were suitably dubbed "WHOOPS bonds" by Wall Street. At the time, it was the largest municipal bond failure in U.S. history.

Although there is much debate as to who or what caused this to happen, why it happened doesn't matter much to investors. According to some reports, a few of the bonds still held the AA rating after the building projects were canceled and six months before the defaults.

A general criticism of bond-rating agencies is that they are too slow to react to changes in an issuer's ability to meet obligations of debt servicing. When a bond defaults, the price collapses as investors sell out. If a rating is lowered, the bond price falls as investors sell out. Even if rating services react swiftly to change the rating, bond prices will drop. To the individual investor, the effect is much the same. All investing has an element of risk, even insured certificates of deposit and T-bills have reinvestment risk (interest rates might go lower). The best one can do to minimize risk with bond investing is to be aware of the current bond rating and remember that ratings can and do change.

BOND RATINGS AGENCIES

Moody's Investor Service

Phone: (212) 553-1653
Internet address: http://www.moodys.com
Mailing address: 99 Church Street, New York, NY 10007

In 1909, John Moody started the first bond ratings as part of Moody's *Analyses of Railroad Investments*. He used the shorthand letter rating Aaa-through-C symbols that became standard designations. The independent rating opinions helped investors better manage credit risk and save time by decreasing the need for painstaking analysis.

If a professional investor has an investment policy limiting bonds to A-rated or better, it is a simple matter to select the proper bonds. If speculators want to invest in bonds, they select either lower-rated or nonrated bonds.

During the Great Depression, when bond default rates were soaring, few highly rated Moody's bonds failed to make payments. Later, during the 1970s, Moody's ratings were expanded to commercial paper and bank deposits.

Standard & Poor's Corporation

Phone: (212) 208-8000
Internet address: http://www.ratings.com

Standard & Poor's Ratings Services is another provider of timely, objective credit analysis and information. Since 1916, S&P has been rating conventional-term debt, general-obligation corporate bonds, and municipal bonds. The familiar letter-grade ratings symbols have long been trusted measures of credit quality worldwide.

Operating without any government mandate, Standard & Poor's also is not connected to an investment banking firm or similar organization. In addition, S&P does not engage in trading or underwriting activities. The company's stated mission is to provide objective, insightful risk analysis and evaluation.

Standard & Poor's was the first analytical organization to publish ratings criteria and procedures as well as the first to introduce an online service—CreditWire—for dissemination of information to the news media and subscribers. They also developed the first print publication dedicated to credit evaluation—Standard & Poor's *CreditWeek*.

Today, Standard & Poor's Ratings Services serves more than 60 countries through a global office network staffed by local analysts from the world's major capital markets.

Fitch Investors Service, L.P.

Phone: (800) 75-FITCH

Internet address: http://www.fitchibca.com

Fitch IBCA is an international rating agency, with dual headquarters in New York and London and a French parent company. The agency maintains established coverage of over 1000 banks and financial institutions, approximately 400 corporations around the world, and 50 sovereigns. The company has a leading market position in structured finance, as well as a developed business in key U.S. markets.

Duff & Phelps Credit Rating Co.

Phone: (312) 368-3100

Internet address: http://www.dcr-ratings.com

Duff & Phelps Credit Rating Co. (DCR) is a local resource for fixed-income issuers, intermediaries, and investors around the world. DCR makes use of its global experience to work in support of local markets. The company has 30-plus local-market offices, which are staffed with skilled rating professionals who have an understanding of local customs and financial conditions.

Table 39-1 compares the respective rankings of the four ratings companies just discussed.

INVESTMENT GRADE

To most conservative investors, ratings of A or better are considered investment grade. Anything less is considered speculative. In general, higher risk does mean higher rewards with bond investing. That is, the lower ratings either tend to pay higher coupon interest or have lower prices. However, the risk is very real and should not be underestimated.

T A B L E 39–1

Ratings System

Classification	S&P	Moody's	Fitch	Duff & Phelps
Prime	AAA	Aaa	AAA	AAA
Maximum safety				
High grade	AA+	Aa1	AA+	AA+
High quality				
	AA	Aa2	AA	AA
	AA–	Aa3	AA–	AA–
Upper-medium	A+	A1	A+	A+
grade	A	A2	A	A
	A–	A3	A–	·A–
Lower-medium	BBB+	Baa1	BBB+	BBB+
grade	BBB	Baa2	BBB	BBB
	BBB–	Baa3	BBB–	BBB–
Noninvestment	BB+	Ba1	BB+	BB+
grade speculative				
	BB	Ba2	BB	BB
	BB–	Ba3	BB–	BB–
Highly speculative	B+	B1	B+	B+
	B	B2	B	B
	B–	B3	B–	B–
Substantial risk	CCC+	Caa	CCC	CCC
Poor standing				
	CCC			
	CCC–			
Extremely		Ca		
speculative				
May be in default		C		
Default			DDD	
			DD	DD
	D		D	
				DP

OBJECTIVITY

Although the bond-rating agencies expend considerable energy and time to keep all evaluations and bond ratings as objective as possible, the human factor introduces a certain amount of subjectivity into the endeavor. Bond issuers actively lobby to convince rating agencies of their good intentions and ability to service debts.

At times, some element of subjectivity may be decisive in obtaining a good rating or in keeping an existing rating strong.

LOOK BEYOND RATINGS

Many investors look beyond the bond ratings and do further financial analysis of the issuing organization. If the issuer is a publicly traded company, analysis of the company's fundamentals and the common stock performance can be informative as to financial strength.

CHAPTER 40

Watch the Consumer Price Index

The Consumer Price Index is essentially the official indicator of inflation. Basic inflation is defined as an increase in prices. The CPI measures the change in price of a "shopping basket" of consumer goods for a given country on a monthly basis. The "core" CPI refers to the change in prices without the food and energy, since their prices are highly volatile. The core CPI is believed to be the accurate measure of inflation.

CPI CALCULATION

An index is a tool to simplify the measurement of movements in a numerical series. Most of the specific CPI indexes have a 1982–1984 reference base, which is updated every 10 years or so. An average index level (representing the average price level) is set for the 36-month period for 1982, 1983, and 1984—equal to 100. Changes are measured in relation to that figure. An index of 110 means there has been a 10% increase in price since the base period. An index of 90 would indicate a 10% decrease from the 100 base period.[1]

---

1 Based on information from "Frequently Asked Questions," the Bureau of Labor Statistics, URL: http://stats.bls.gov/cpifaq.htm, 1998.

ADJUSTED OR UNADJUSTED

Data on the Consumer Price Index is available in either seasonally adjusted or unadjusted versions. To observe the escalation of inflation, the unadjusted data is recommended as a more accurate view.

THE CPI AND 10-YEAR TREASURY BOND YIELDS

To compare the CPI to something familiar, Figure 40–1 shows the growth of the CPI in relation to the 10-year bond yields from 1968 to 1998 (through October). Keeping in mind the base of 100 for the 1982–1984 time period, the index is calculated back to 1968.

F I G U R E 40–1

Inflation, Consumer Price Index and 10-Year, 1968–1998

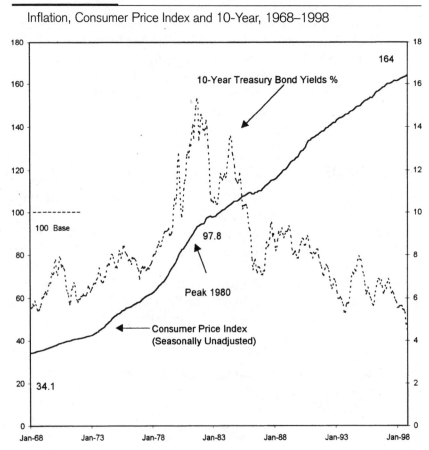

FIGURE 40–2

Inflation, Consumer Price Index and 10-Year Treasury Bond Yields, 1979–1981

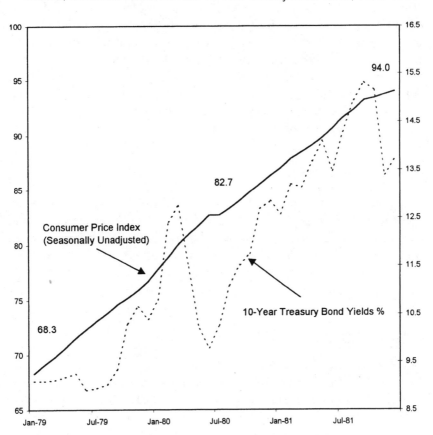

Notice the acceleration of the curve in the "inflationary spiral" of the 1960s to early 1980s. Inflation peaked in 1980, rising 13.5% for that year.[2] Yields on Treasury bonds peaked the following November, with the 10-year yield at 15.32%. Clearly, inflation was proving difficult to control.

2 Thomas M. Hoenig, President, Federal Reserve Bank of Kansas City, Kansas City, Missouri, "Three Lessons for Monetary Policy," remarks to the Fed Correspondents Association, New York, NY, April 22, 1998, http://www.kc.frb.org/spch&bio/ hoenig49.htm.

After a slight hesitation in July 1980, the CPI resumed its upward course. The angle of ascent is less, but not much less. Figure 40–2 shows that hesitation clearly. Notice the surprising volatility of the bond yield in mid-1980. The bond yield dropped nearly 3%. Is it any wonder the CPI would resume its climb? Although it's possible to stimulate the economy with lower interest rates or restrict the economy (and inflation) with higher interest rates, they can't be done simultaneously. Since 1980 was an election year (Carter versus Reagan), interest rates were probably lowered to dress up the economy before the election.

WHAT ABOUT NOW?

A comparison of high inflation to a period of low inflation shows interest rates can be low and inflation relatively under control at the same time. Figure 40–3 shows the 10-year yield dropping from 6.91% to 4.53%, while inflation did not appear to accelerate. The CPI rose 9.3 points in the 1996–1998 period, while the 1979–1981 period experienced a CPI increase of 25.6 points.

A MORE AGGRESSIVE FED

On April 22, 1998, Thomas M. Hoenig, President of the Federal Reserve Bank of Kansas City, Missouri, made a presentation to the Fed Correspondents' Association in New York. The title of his presentation was "Three Lessons for Monetary Policy." Essentially, Mr. Hoenig was addressing the management of inflation. To paraphrase his main points, or "lessons":

1. Don't let the inflation process get started.
2. Don't rely only on a single indicator to make decisions on monetary policy.
3. Keep the long-run objective of price stability always in mind.

The Federal Reserve Bank wants the economy to be stable and growing. They do not want it to become inflationary and unstable. An annual inflation rate of 2% to 3% is necessary to sustain economic growth. Interest rates on the low side also help the economy grow by reducing the cost of doing business.

FIGURE 40–3

Inflation, Consumer Price Index and 10-Year, 1996–1998

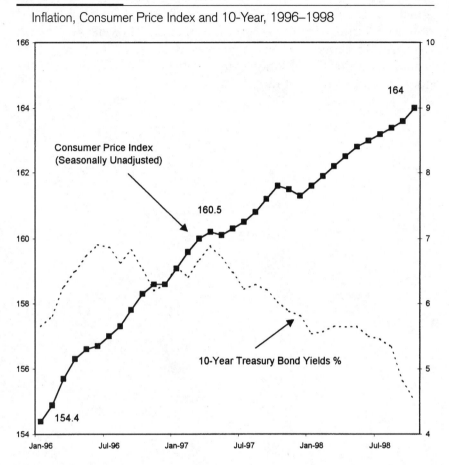

CPI MONTHLY

The Consumer Price Index is issued by the Bureau of Labor Statistics on a monthly basis. Many times, the bond and stock markets anticipate the monthly report and discount its changes ahead of time. At other times, the report contains surprises and becomes the cause of sudden volatility.

AN INDICATOR

The CPI is an indicator of inflation in the economy. By following its progress, the individual bond investor can develop some understanding of where interest rates are heading. If there is a sudden interest rate increase, is it a preemptive strike on the part of the Fed to halt inflation, or will it become a tightening of money to slow an overheating economy? News reports relating to such increases usually examine the situation extensively and can give the investor good insights into what might happen next.

CHAPTER 41

Insured Municipal Bonds Are Safer

Bond insurance can be attached to virtually any issued bond—municipal, corporate, and so on. The insurance guarantees the timely payment of interest and principal if the issuer of the bond defaults. Insured bonds are normally given a rating of AAA, the highest possible from the rating services. Here we select municipal bond insurance as an example.

MUNICIPAL BOND INSURANCE

Insurance policies protect investors if a municipal bond doesn't pay (defaults). Two major insurers of municipal bonds are the Ambac Indemnity Corporation (AMBAC) and the Municipal Bond Insurance Association (MBIA). Insured municipal bonds usually have the highest ratings (AAA). Because of the high rating, the bond's marketability increases, which lowers the cost to the issuer. Insurance costs, however, so the yield on an insured bond is lower than similarly rated uninsured bonds. In this way, the cost of the insurance is passed on to the investor. Investors buying insured bonds are willing to accept a lower yield for higher safety against default.

WHAT DOESN'T INSURANCE COVER?

Insurance of this kind does not cover market risk. If interest rates rise, the price of a bond issued at a lower yield will drop. For most investors, this only becomes a problem if it becomes necessary to sell the bonds. Held to maturity, the bonds will still return the face value. This is guaranteed by the insurance.

TOO MUCH INSURANCE

Many people like to hear the word *insured* when referring to investments. Perhaps this is because they are used to having insurance on federally insured bank accounts and certificates of deposit. The word is so important to some people that they prefer insured certificates of deposit to Treasury bills, notes, and bonds. They believe, erroneously, that the certificates are safer because they are insured.

It seems like too much to have insurance on a closed-end unit trust of municipal bonds. Municipal unit trusts are made up of several different issues of bonds, so they are diversified. The possibility of several issues going into default is small. Why sacrifice yield for protection when the risk is not very high? Where some of these high-risk trusts might need the insurance, others might have only wanted to sell the bonds as quickly as possible.

For new municipal bond issues, the insurance stays with the bonds for the life of the bond. For unit investment trusts, there can be two types of insurance: either permanent, for the life of the bond, or for as long as a bond stays in the unit trust.[1]

HOW MUCH DOES INSURANCE COST?

Comparing the yield on an insured bond to other similar bonds with the same maturity will give some idea of the insurance cost. The comparison can be difficult, because it depends on availability and it's not always easy to match the parameters. Bond insurance will normally lower the yield by up to one quarter of a percent (25 basis points). For this additional cost of insurance, credit risk is eliminated.

---

1 Although unit trusts are not "managed" or traded, substitutions or replacements are sometimes made.

LISTING SERVICE

Another way to evaluate an insured bond yield is to compare it to a national yield listing service such as the Internet service maintained by Zia Corporation (http//www.callzia.com). Zia is a software development company, dealing with institutional investors and dealers. They also provide listings of municipal bonds from a variety of brokerage firms. The listings include a bond rating, description, coupon percentage, and an offer price, which is either stated as a percent of face value or current yield (coupon dollar amount divided by price). Of course, prices can change during the next trading session, depending on the market.

For example, on April 30, 1999, Zia listed some ten-year Michigan building revenue bonds with a coupon of 5.2% and a current yield of 4.4%, insured by Ambac. How does the issue compare to the national scale? On Zia's scale, a ten-year insured bond is normally going for a current yield of 4.4%, so the Michigan bond appears to be on target. Again, it must be stressed that individual bond prices for munis can have unique qualities, which change their value. When doing a comparison, oftentimes the best you can hope for is a ballpark figure.

SAFER THAN WHAT?

Are insured bonds safer? This begs another question: Safer than what? The principal and interest payments of insured bonds are safer than if they were not insured. Are insured bonds safer than those with AA or AAA ratings? Possibly not, at least in most situations. Although there can be defaults in highly rated bonds, the probability is low. That is why they have the high credit ratings.

CHAPTER 42

Watch the Long Bond

Many investors, individual and professional, believe the long bond to be one of the best indicators of where interest rates are going. If the long bond has the most volatile prices, logically it would also have the most volatile yields and would likely be first to react to economic changes.

INTEREST RATES RISE

When interest rates rise, money becomes tighter and the economy slows. At times, rates are intentionally raised to cause a small slowdown rather than have inflation get out of control and cause a recession.

The 30-year bond yield is an interest rate and one of the most volatile. If the long bond yield rises, many believe it is forecasting an economic slowdown (Figure 42–1).

The rising 30-year yields in 1979 and 1980 certainly appeared to forecast a weakness in the gross domestic product that appeared in mid-1980. Yields appear to have been quickly lowered to offer some stimulation, and the weakness only lasted until December. After that, we see how much of a problem interest rates can be. Although the rates keep rising, the GDP takes a long time to slow. It takes from June of 1980 until October of 1981 to see a turn.

F I G U R E 42–1

Economic Slowdown, 30-Year Bond and GDP, 1979–1983

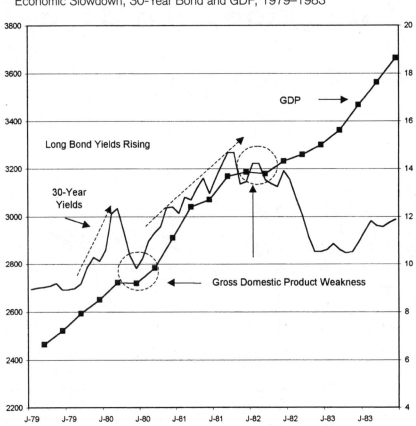

OTHER INFLATION FACTORS

Inflation is concerned with more factors than just long bond yields
and the gross domestic product. There is also the upward spiral of
wages and prices. In many ways, they are a larger concern.
Controlling wages and prices is not easily accomplished in an open
economy. It has been tried, but success was limited and temporary.
It's usually easier to control interest rates and the money supply.
That is why the yield on the long bond has some forecasting tendencies, especially where a trend is established.

F I G U R E 42–2

Economic Stimulation, 30-Year Bond and GDP, 1979–1983

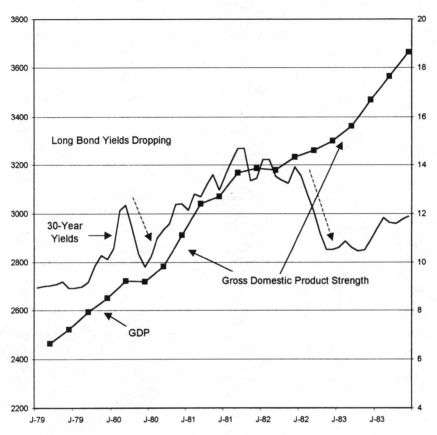

INTEREST RATES DROP

If rising interest rates slow the economy and cause the GDP to weaken, it's only logical that a drop in rates will strengthen the gross domestic product (Figure 42–2).

The GDP regains strength quickly, as can be seen in 1980 and again in 1982. Strength can return by the next quarter. In June of 1982, with inflation believed to be under control, interest rates were lowered again. They stayed down until May of 1983, when another uptrend began.

FIGURE 42-3

Economic Stimulation, 30-Year Bond and GDP, 1996–1998

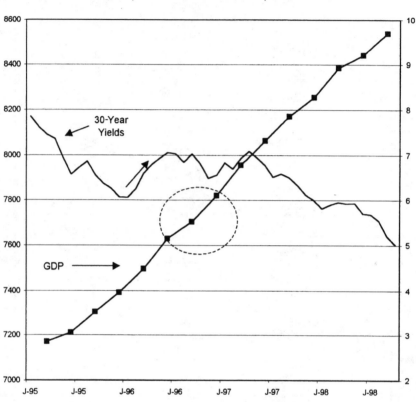

WHAT ABOUT 1998?

Figures 42–1 and 42–2 showed the forecasting ability of the long bond yield, based on information from 1979 to 1983. The years were selected because they showed some clear impact. If we look at a chart from 1996–1998, the impact exists but is not so dramatic (Figure 42–3).

Notice how the interest rates (yields) are considerably lower than in the earlier years. During 1979–1983, long bond yields were between 9% and 14.68%. In the more recent years, the highest yield was less than 8%.

NOT THE ONLY INDICATOR

Although trends in the yield of the long bond can be an indicator of economic strength or weakness, it should never be the only indicator used. It is a quick indicator one can easily reference or track.

CHAPTER 43

You Can't Trade Bonds Like Stocks

Although there are some professional traders and individuals who attempt to trade bonds on a regular basis, there are some serious difficulties involved with analysis, tracking data, and price transparency.

With common stocks, analysis can be performed on revenues, earnings, p/e ratios, and most important, price data. With bonds, although government and municipal bonds have shown some improvement, information on corporate bond transactions often is not made available to the public.

SEC CHAIRMAN TESTIFIES

On September 29, 1998, Securities and Exchange Commission Chairman Arthur Levitt testified before the House Subcommittee on Finance and Hazardous Materials, Committee on Commerce, concerning transparency in the U.S. debt market.[1] Two recommendations were made to improve corporate bond trading:

> First, adopt rules requiring dealers to report all transactions in U.S. corporate bonds and preferred stocks to the NASD and to develop systems to receive and redistribute transaction prices on an immediate basis.
>
> Second, create a database of transactions in corporate bonds and preferred stocks.

---

1 The full text of Mr. Levitt's testimony can be found on the Internet at http://www.sec.gov/ news/testmony/tsty1398.htm.

WHAT ARE THEY TRYING TO IMPROVE?

Fairness to all investors and traders alike, that's what's needed in the current global trading markets. To create that level playing field, where all participants can have access to the same information at the same time, stock exchanges and self-regulatory organizations like the National Association of Securities Dealers are charged with creating a market that is "fair and orderly."

SEC REQUEST

The SEC is requesting that the National Association of Securities Dealers (NASD) do three things:

> First, require dealers to report all U.S. corporate bond transactions to the NASD and immediately redistribute the information.
>
> Second, establish a transaction database for U.S. corporate bonds and preferred stocks, which will assist in supervising the corporate debt market.
>
> Third, using the database, establish a surveillance program to detect fraud.

LIQUIDITY AND CONFUSION CONCERNS

Concerns of some people over this information becoming available are that it might affect the liquidity (ease of buying and selling) or might be confusing to investors. These concerns were also voiced when changes were made in government securities and municipal markets, but they were not a problem. The SEC further believes the widespread availability of prices from transactions will improve day-end valuations.

WILL BONDS TRADE LIKE STOCKS?

The SEC claims they are not intending to impose a trading system like the one that has developed for stock. Rather, their concern and goal is to protect the interest of investors by "tailoring requirements" in bond market operations. An important example is the fact that stocks trade with continuous quotations, whereas corporate bond dealers don't generally publish "firm quotes."

The SEC is not proposing to change this unless the market develops in that direction. Maybe it will. Witness this press release from the Bank of New York:

Institutional Investors Begin Using Electronic Bond Trading
New York, NY, April 8, 1998—The Bank of New York announced today that it has completed the initial installation of its electronic bond trading system, BondNet, with a group of large institutional investors. Additional installations are scheduled for the next few weeks with many more likely in the future as investors embrace electronic bond trading.[2]

The press release went on to say that the BondNet system provides automated trade matching and order routing, real-time pricing and market information, and analytic and order management functions.

Furthermore, using the BondNet system, buyers and sellers can match or negotiate live bids and offers, distribute and analyze inventory, and conduct trades on an instantaneous and anonymous basis.

The future may already be here.

---

2 The Bank of New York Company, Inc., Rev: July 30, 1998, http://www.bankofny.com/pressrel/elecbond.htm.

CHAPTER 44

Bonds Always Mature at Par

Well, of course they do. Why bother with a statement of the obvious? Because investors can be carried away with bonds trading at a premium. A few of them might even believe they will be paid more than par at maturity. But they won't receive more, no matter how high the price goes. Reality usually sets in as maturity is approached and the bond price comes down to its par value.

PAR VALUE IS FACE VALUE

The word *par* comes from Latin and means *equal to*. When referring to bonds it means equal to the face value of the bonds. The face value of most bonds is $1000, no more and no less.

MATURE OR CALLED

When bonds mature, the face value (par) is returned to the current bondowner. The bonds might be called by the issuer, meaning the issuer will be returning the face value before the maturity date. Issuers do this to take advantage of lower interest rates on their bonds. The old bonds are called and repaid; then new bonds with lower yields are issued.

BONDS MATURE AT PAR

Whether it's called par, face value, or $1000, this is what most bonds return to the investor on the maturity date.

CHAPTER 45

If a Yield Looks Too Good to Be True, It Probably Is

If someone rents a storefront in any major metropolitan area and puts a sign in the window saying something like INSURED CDs 15% when bank certificates of deposit are at 5%, a crowd of people will gather to inquire. It's almost a guarantee. Hopefully, a crowd of law enforcement officers will also gather and put a stop to the nonsense.

A NASTY SECRET

One of the tricks of "hot shot" junk bond jockeys is to get someone on the phone and let them "overhear" an imaginary conversation they are having in which an unusually high percentage yield is stated. The salesperson then puts the prospect (sucker) on hold, just to let her or him think about that high yield. When the salesperson returns to the telephone, the prospect is often champing at the bit to get the high-yield investment. Caution and risk considerations are quickly forgotten. High yield is everything, to earn a higher income. Forget risk. Forget these damnable low yields. Let's make some income. Let's take a "flyer." All too often, the flyer suddenly crashes and the investor is left with nothing.

HIGH YIELD MEANS HIGHER RISK

Especially the very high yield. The only way to dramatically increase yield on fixed-income investing is to increase the risk. Moderate increases can come from extending maturity dates or slightly increasing risk, but truly high yields always means taking on high risk. That's why we so often hear, "If it sounds too good to be true, it probably is."

BEST STRATEGY

Instead of waiting on hold, hang up the phone. At the very least, insist that the sales representative send out information before a decision is reached.

Beware of Personal Guarantees

When it comes to the market safety, success, or failure of any investment, no one can personally guarantee success. It's unethical and usually illegal. To invest money means to place money at risk. If there were no risk involved, there would be no investment. It would be a simple business transaction—and not offered to the public.

FEARS TOO GREAT

Sometimes investors' fear of losing money is too high, so high they end up taking a high risk, possibly based on a personal guarantee. Then they lose everything. News reports every year present stories in which investors have lost thousands and hundreds of thousands of dollars based on the personal guarantee of someone they trusted. In many cases, the culprit had been a friend for several years.

IT CAN HAPPEN TO ANYONE

Shortly before his death, President Ulysses S. Grant lost virtually all of his money based on a guarantee of his son's friend. In early June of 1884, his fortune, which only a few months earlier had been worth more than $2 million, suddenly shrank to some $80 in cash.

His widow became financially secure only after the publication of Grant's memoirs.[1]

INVESTING MONEY NEEDS TRANSPARENCY

Investing should never amount to giving someone a small or modest pile of money in hope of having a large pile of money returned. Prices need to be known before the investor makes a trade. Buy or sell transactions need to occur, with confirmations spelling out the details. Statements need to be received, informing investors of changes in their account status. Investors need to know what's going on in their accounts. That is what statements tell them. Someone's personal guarantee isn't good enough anymore. Investors need information they can see and verify.

---

1 *The Gilded Age,* published in 1885 by the Charles L. Webster Company, a Mark Twain concern.

CHAPTER 47

Know the Types of Bonds

U.S. GOVERNMENT TREASURY ISSUES

These bonds are backed by the full faith and credit of the U.S. federal government. They are exempt from state and local taxes.

Treasury Bills

T-bills are short-term investments. They mature in 13 weeks, 26 weeks, or 1 year. In the past, T-bills cost at least $10,000, but that has now been lowered to a $1000 minimum investment.

Treasury Notes

Notes, which are medium-term, mature in 2 to 10 years and pay interest twice a year. The minimum investment is $1000.

Treasury Bonds

Treasury bonds mature in 10 to 30 years and pay interest semiannually. The minimum required for a Treasury bond is $1000.

Zero-Coupon Treasuries (Short-, Medium-, Long-term)

Zeroes pay no interest until maturity. You can purchase a zero at a large discount from face value. They mature in anywhere from a few months to several years.

Treasury Inflation-Protected Securities (TIPS)

TIPS are newer Treasury bonds in which changes in the price are determined by the changes in the Consumer Price Index (CPI). The bonds have 10- and 30-year maturities and require a minimum investment of $1000.

MUNICIPAL ISSUES

Also called munis, these bonds are issued by state and local governments. They normally require $5000 (a five-bond minimum) and over and are free from federal taxes. If you live in the area that issues the muni bond, you usually do not have to pay local or state taxes. That's often referred to as "triple tax-exempt."

General Obligation (GO)

Bonds for the payment of which the full faith and credit of the issuing municipal governments are pledged. These muni bonds allow the municipality to raise taxes to make payments.

Revenue Bonds

Payments of principal and interest depend exclusively on the revenues generated by the facility involved. The bonds do not pledge payment based on the full faith and credit of the issuer. They are also frequently secured by a mortgage on the revenue-producing facilities.

Taxable Municipal Bonds/Industrial Development Bonds

Some munis are issued taxable, with the funds being used for special development projects that the federal government does not consider tax exempt. They are projects that don't benefit the public at large. Investor-led housing, local sports facilities, refunding of a refunded issue and borrowing for a municipality's underfunded pension plan are four types of bond issues that are federally taxable. As one might expect, taxable municipals offer yields comparable to other taxable bonds, such as corporates or agencies.

MORTGAGE-BACKED BONDS

These bonds represent ownership of mortgage loans, which are issued or backed by such government agencies as the Government National Mortgage Association (GNMA). They are not tax-exempt. Mortgage-backed bonds do not gain much value when interest rates go lower. When interest rates decline, homeowners tend to refinance lower rates. Mortgage-backed bonds can require a minimum outlay of $25,000.

CORPORATE ISSUES

Corporate bond interest payments are fully taxable. As they are issued by individual companies, their reliability of paying interest and principal depends on the issuing company. The safest are rated investment-grade, and the riskiest are junk bonds, or high-yield issues, which have no rating. Bond credit ratings are supplied by ratings agencies like Standard & Poor's, Moody's, and Fitch.

FOREIGN BONDS

Foreign bonds are very sensitive to changes in the monetary exchange rate. If the value of the dollar increases, the bonds also increase in value. They can help add diversification to a bond portfolio because interest rates in other countries do not match those of the U.S.

BRADY BONDS

Brady Bonds were issued by third-world nations such as Mexico, Brazil, and Argentina as they restructured their debt under a plan developed by former U.S. Treasury Secretary Nicholas Brady. The principal on some of the bonds and 12 to 18 months of interest payments are backed by U.S. Treasury securities.

CHAPTER 48

Consider a Managed Futures Account

Until the 1980s, futures market participants were hedgers and speculators. The 1980s experienced the advent of a third major market participant, the managed futures investor. Like a futures speculator, the managed futures investor seeks to profit from price movement. However, unlike the speculator, the managed futures investor employs a third-party decision maker known as a *commodity trading advisor* (CTA).

WHY TRADE IN MANAGED FUTURES?

Investors' interest in new global markets and willingness to accept the potential benefits of professionals (the CTAs trading their accounts) have contributed greatly to the growth of managed futures.

While it is popular for individuals to invest in the stock and bond markets, it is not as common for individuals to invest in futures markets. It is difficult for individuals to successfully trade in futures markets. The U.S. government has conducted studies suggesting that as many as 90% of individuals who trade futures and make their own buy and sell decisions end up losing money.

REWARD-RISK ONE-WAY STREET

With investing, as the potential reward goes higher, the potential risk increases too. However, it's a one-way street. If risk is increased, it doesn't necessarily mean that rewards will also go higher.

RISK AND REWARD

The relationship in investing between risk and reward is usually measured by volatility, the up and down swings of securities prices. Futures tend to be highly volatile, with the potential for greater returns and the possibility of significant losses.

Generally, increased returns have increased volatility. An investor must decide on an acceptable comfort zone of risk-reward and stay within it, even though this might be difficult. Figures 48–1 and 48–2 depict stocks, bonds, and managed futures investments in terms of their risk-reward (volatility) characteristics.

The first visual clearly illustrates the higher-reward-means-higher-volatility concept. Volatility can indeed mean higher risk. Volatility means prices oscillate between extremes of high and low. While many investors can resist the temptation to sell on a high swing, the emotional impact of a severe decline frequently causes them to take losses. Obviously, there comes a time when losses must be taken. Assets have to be repositioned in the attempt to recoup and recover. However, when investing in investment

F I G U R E 48–1

Volatility Tends to Increase with Return

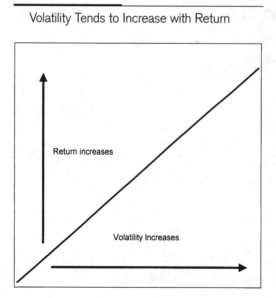

Return increases

Volatility Increases

FIGURE 48–2

Volatility Tends to Increase with Return and
Investment Class

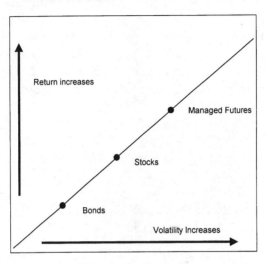

classes that have a higher level of volatility, one must be careful
and not sell too soon. In other words, don't judge the volatility of
futures by the same standards used for common stock or bond
volatility.

Figure 48–2 illustrates that higher rewards and higher risk
tend to accompany each other. The illustration is to make the point
that the different classes of investment have increasing rewards
and volatility. It does not mean to suggest that the rewards and
volatility increase at a steady rate. It just means managed futures
tend to have greater returns and volatility than stocks, which in
turn have greater returns and volatility than bonds.

PORTFOLIO VOLATILITY

To the investor diversified into bonds, common stock, and managed futures, the rewards and volatility are moderated. Although
the futures portion of the portfolio is the most speculative, the risk
is lessened and the volatility is lowered by the funds invested in
bonds and stock. The point is this: The portfolio opportunity for
higher gains is enhanced by the managed futures segment.

SPECULATIVE FUNDS ONLY

Any futures trading should not be done with funds where preservation of capital is of the highest order. Futures trading is for speculative funds. There is still risk involved, even for the experts. However, it can be a reasonably prudent way to increase the return on an investment portfolio that can afford to take some risk. Because of the risks involved, futures trading has minimum income and net worth requirements to determine suitability.

OBTAIN INFORMATION

Further information on futures can be obtained from the exchanges:

Chicago Board of Trade (CBOT)
141 West Jackson Boulevard
Chicago, IL 60604-2994
Phone: (312) 435-3500
Internet Address: www.cbot.com

Chicago Mercantile Exchange (CME)
30 South Wacker Drive
Chicago, IL 60606
Phone: (312) 930-1000
Internet Address: www.cme.com

New York Mercantile Exchange
One North End Avenue
World Financial Center
New York, NY 10282-1101
Phone: (212) 299-2000

CHAPTER 49

Buy Brady Bonds for High Yields

The introduction of Brady bonds was the direct outcome of the Brady Plan implementation, which aimed at reducing debt in emerging countries. During the 1980s, debt negotiations focused on new private lending and debt restructuring. As this approach was not solving the debt crisis, the Bush administration, through Secretary of the Treasury Nicholas Brady, put forth a new plan for reducing debt. Under the plan, debt was reduced in recognition that the market value of the commercial bank loans was less than face value. The loans were restructured as publicly traded, U.S. dollar-denominated bonds generally referred to as "Brady bonds."

TYPES OF BRADY BONDS

Brady bond issues include a number of different bond types. Although par bonds and discount bonds account for the majority of the Brady bonds issued to date, countries have issued substantial numbers of bonds that differ significantly from pars and discounts, especially in terms of the degree of collateralization.

PAR BONDS

A *par bond* is issued and redeemed at par, that usually being a price of 100% of face value, like a coupon bond. After issue, the par bond price varies inversely with changes in interest rates. When interest rates go up, the bond price goes down. United States Treasury bonds and notes are examples of this type of security.

DISCOUNT BONDS

Discounts are bonds issued at a deep discount. They mature at face value, like zero-coupon bonds.

SOME BRADY BOND EXAMPLES

Collateralized Bonds

Mexican Par Bonds

With Brady bonds, the par bond face value equals the principal value of the commercial loans they replaced, but they carry reduced fixed-rate coupons. The coupons can remain fixed or be subject to a step-up provision, where the interest rate increases according to a prearranged schedule.

Mexican par bonds were issued in March 1990, with 29¾-year maturities and fixed 6¼% coupons. As with other Brady bonds, they are dollar-denominated, with their principal assured by zero-coupon U.S. Treasury bonds. Although there exist a Series A and Series B, currently, there are no differences in the two that can affect the present value of their income streams. Series A and Series B par bonds trade as a single issue.

Guarantee Fund

Like most par bonds, Mexican par bonds also have access to a fund of high-grade, short-term securities designated to guarantee a number of interest payments (normally 6 to 18 months). Despite their par designation, the bonds were issued at a price below their face value. The term *par* is used in reference to the fact that at the date of issue, the face value of these bonds was equal to the value of outstanding loans they replaced.

Noncollateralized Bonds

Argentine Floating Rate Bonds (FRBs); Brazilian C Bonds, and Eligible Interest (EI) Bonds

Perhaps the most important difference between Mexican par bonds and issues from Argentina and Brazil is the collateralization. In contrast to Mexican par bonds, Brazil's eligible interest bonds (EIs) and front-loaded interest reduction with capitalization option bonds (C bonds) have no collateral guarantees. The prices of these bonds reflect the market's opinion of the present value payments to be made over the life of the bond. In contrast, the price of a Mexican par bond is made up of two parts: a collateralized component and a stream of payments over the life of the bond.

Coupons among the bonds differ also. Mexican pars, Argentine FRBs, and Brazilian Cs and EIs all pay interest on a semiannual basis. However, whereas Mexican pars pay a fixed 6¼% coupon, the Brazilian Cs pay a fixed-rate coupon that increases in steps over time. Brazilian EIs and Argentine FRBs pay a floating-rate coupon based on six-month LIBOR (London Inter-Bank Offered Rate), plus 1⅜%.

The maturities and repayment schedules vary also. Argentine FRBs and Brazilian bonds repay their principal components in semiannual installments during the last 9 to 10 years of the bond's life. Mexican par bonds repay the entire principal at maturity. The maturities of Argentine FRBs and Brazilian EIs are fairly close to each other: March 31, 2005, for the FRBs and April 15, 2006, for the EIs. Brazilian C bonds mature on April 15, 2014, and Mexican par bonds on December 31, 2019.[1]

COMPLICATED

There can be complications in buying any foreign bonds, but the Brady bonds appear to have more than usual. Obviously, there are many variables to the structure, payment, and collateralization of the bonds.

COUNTRIES WITH BRADY BONDS

Several countries are involved with Brady Plan restructuring, among them Argentina, Brazil, Bulgaria, Costa Rica, Croatia, Dominican Republic, Ecuador, Mexico, Morocco, Nigeria, Panama, Peru, Philippines, Poland, Russia, Slovenia, Uruguay, and Venezuela.

---

1 Based on 1998 information from the Chicago Mercantile Exchange, where futures on
   Brady bonds are traded.

HIGH YIELD

According to JP Morgan Bond indices, returns can be high one year and low the next. The year after the creation of Brady bonds (1991) showed:

Brazil	36.26%
Mexico	38.95%
Venezuela	39.78%

However, 1992 was distinctly different:

Brazil	–1.56%
Mexico	13.61%
Venezuela	–9.65%

Later, in 1995, things looked better:

Brazil	20.49%
Mexico	25.86%
Venezuela	41.05%

Considering that the motivation to establish the concept of Brady bonds was to assist debt-laden countries, it's not surprising to see volatility. Investors are buying the bonds for high yield and price swings. With high risk, any negative news can place security prices in jeopardy. Although debt can be an important factor of economic stability, it is not the only one.

HIGH VOLATILITY

Brazil's currency devaluation in 1999 sent the United States stock markets into a frenzy. During the second week of January, Brazil's decision to devalue its currency had an impact on much of the world. On the fifteenth of January, this is what some of Brazil's Brady bonds looked like:

Brazilian Brady Bonds			
Issue	Bid	Offer	Cash-Flow Yield
IDU	85.75	86.75	19.73%
EI	62.00	63.00	19.69%
MYDFA 2007	53.50	55.50	25.24%
FLIRB	43.00	48.00	21.37%
NMB	52.00	54.00	20.66%
EXIT	60.00	70.00	15.03%
DCB	46.50	48.00	18.85%
CBOND	56.00	57.00	17.12%
PAR	55.00	56.00	11.33%
DISC	55.00	56.00	12.20%
GLOBAL01	84.00	88.00	15.19%
BNDES	63.50	65.50	17.17%
BR GLO 08	63.50	65.50	17.17%
GLOBAL27	62.00	64.00	16.17%

Data source: BradyNet.

There are some high yields for perceived high risk. The bid here is what an investor could sell a bond for, stated as a percentage of face value. The offer would be an investor's buy price, also stated as a percentage of face value.

International investing always has its surprises. Problems appear one day and are gone the next. When an investor buys the actual securities, there can be many surprises. A gain of more than 38% for a year can be a pleasant surprise; however, a loss of 27% or more would not be pleasant.

KNOW THE INVESTMENT

Brady bonds have many variations in type, payment, maturity, and collateralization. To add bonds like this to a diversified portfolio, the investor needs to learn the differences. Does this bond have collateral? How does it pay back principal? Is the bond rated? Is the country rated for credit risk? Ask the questions and get some answers. It might help avoid additional unpleasant surprises when the bonds reach maturity.

CHAPTER 50

Learn the Language of Bonds

Accrued Interest The amount of interest to be paid the buyer of a bond on a purchase completed between interest payment dates. Accrued interest is effectively returned as the investor receives the full coupon payment.

AMT Bonds The interest from certain tax-free municipal bonds is required to be included in the calculation of alternative minimum tax. These bonds are generally referred to as AMT bonds

Asset Allocation The division of investment money into percentages of money market, capital appreciation (stocks), and fixed-income (bonds). Asset allocation is done for diversification and market advantage.

Barbell Portfolio A common strategy for investing in bonds of differing maturities to hedge against fluctuations in interest rates. Some money is invested in short-term and some in long-term bonds. The strategy enables the investor to take advantage of higher yields long-term yet participate in interest rate increases on the short side of the barbell.

Basis Point A basis point is one one-hundredth of a percent ($\frac{1}{100}$% or .01%). Yield differences between fixed-income securities are stated in basis points. (For example, the difference between a bond yielding 5.0% and one yielding 5.15% is 15 basis points.)

Bearer Bond A bearer bond is one that is not registered by the issuer. The issuer has no identification of an owner. It is owned by the bearer. Because they are easily lost or stolen, most financial firms require some form of proof of ownership to sell these bonds.

Brady Bond These are bonds issued by third-world nations, such as Mexico, Brazil, and Argentina, when they restructured their debt under a plan developed by former U.S. Treasury Secretary Nicholas Brady. The principal of many bonds as well as 12 to 18 months of interest payments of some is backed by U.S. Treasury securities.

Callable Bond   Callable bonds are redeemable by the issuer prior to the stated maturity date. A call date and price are specified. Bonds are likely to be called if interest rates drop.

Call Premium   A dollar amount, usually specified as a percentage of the face value being redeemed, paid as a "premium" for redeeming early.

Certificate of Deposit (CD)   A certificate issued for a deposit made at a banking institution. The bank agrees to pay a fixed interest rate for a specific time and repays the principal at the maturity. CDs can be purchased directly from the banking institution or through a securities broker.

Collateralized Bond   Bonds backed by the assets that the issuer puts up as collateral for the issue, such as real estate holdings or equipment. Usually this refers to a type of corporate bond.

Collateralized Mortgage Obligation (CMO)   A bond backed by a pool of mortgage pass-through securities or mortgage loans.

Convertible Bond   A corporate bond that can be exchanged for shares of the issuer's common stock at a specific exchange ratio and price.

Corporate Bonds   Debt obligations issued by private or public companies to raise funds for a variety of corporate purposes, such as building a new facility, purchasing equipment, or expanding the business.

Coupon   Usually refers to a bond's stated interest rate based on face value. Coupons are generally paid every six months.

Consumer Price Index (CPI-U)   The seasonally unadjusted U.S. City Average All Items Consumer Price Index for All Urban Consumers, published by the Bureau of Labor Statistics. Based on a "basket" of goods and services, it is considered to be a measure of an increase or decrease in inflation.

Current Yield   The rate of actual cash flow as a percentage of the purchase price. It is calculated by dividing the annual interest dollars received on the bond by its purchase price.

CUSIP   Committee on Uniform Securities Identification Procedures: a nine-digit identifier number for a security that is used to maintain a uniform method of identifying municipal, corporate, and U.S. government securities.

Dated Date   The date on a bond issue from which interest starts accruing. The bondholder receives interest from the issuer starting from this date, although the bonds may actually be delivered on a later date.

Debenture Bond   Debentures are corporate bonds that are backed by the good faith of the company issuing the bond. Since there is no collateral, these bonds generally carry a higher risk and therefore a higher yield than a collateralized bond.

Default   Failure to pay principal or interest promptly when due.

Discount   The discount is the difference between a bond's current market price and its face, or redemption, value.

Discount Rate   The rate of interest charged by the Federal Reserve Banks on money borrowed by member banks.

Diversification   The practice of including in a portfolio different types of assets in order to minimize risk or improve performance. An example is to include bonds of different issuers, differing maturities, and various credit qualities in one portfolio.

Double Exemption   Securities, usually tax-free municipal bonds, that are exempt from state income tax as well as federal income taxation. Many states exempt interest earned on bonds issued by political subdivisions within the state.

Federal National Mortgage Association (FNMA)   Also known as "Fannie Mae," it is a U.S. government-sponsored private corporation authorized to purchase and sell home mortgages. FNMA facilitates the orderly operation of the secondary market for these mortgages.

Federal Home Loan Mortgage Corporation (FHLMC)   Also known as "Freddie Mac," this is a federally created corporation that facilitates the financing of single-family residential housing by creating and maintaining an active market for conventional home mortgages.

General Obligation (GO) Bonds   Municipal bonds backed by the full faith and credit (taxing and borrowing power) of the municipality issuing the bonds. If it becomes necessary, the issuer can raise taxes to make payments on the bonds.

Government National Mortgage Association (GNMA)   Also referred to as "Ginnie Mae," this agency of the U.S. Department of Housing and Urban Development is empowered to provide assistance in financing home mortgages. GNMA is responsible for management and liquidation of federally owned mortgage portfolios and issues bonds that are secured by single-family mortgages and guaranteed by the full faith and credit of the U.S. government.

Hedge   To hedge is to offset investment risk in a particular security with another investment or transaction in another market. For example, long position in a bond may be hedged with a put on those bonds. A "perfect hedge" has no loss and no gain potential.

Institutional Investor   A professional organization investing in securities for the benefit of others. Insurance companies, pension funds, investment managers, and mutual funds are institutional investors.

Insured Bonds   Many municipal bonds are backed by municipal bond insurance that is specifically designed to reduce investment risk. In default, the insurance company guarantees payment of principal and interest to the investors for as long as the default lasts. Insured bonds normally carry the highest-quality credit rating, AAA.

Interest   Compensation paid to a lender (investor) by the borrower (issuer of bonds) for the use of money. Interest is usually expressed as an annual percentage rate and is most often paid every six months.

Investment Grade   Bonds graded Baa and higher by Moody's Investors Service and Fitch Investors Service, or BBB and higher by Standard and Poor's, are considered to have only minor speculative characteristics.

Issuer   The issuer is the entity borrowing money through the issuance of bonds. It can be a state; a political subdivision; an agency or authority, in the case of municipal bonds; a corporation, for corporate and agency bonds; or the U.S. government, for Treasury bonds.

Junk Bond   A bond rated lower than Baa/BBB. Also called high-yield bonds, they are considered speculative compared with investment-grade bonds.

Liquidity   The measure of the ease or difficulty with which securities can be bought and sold in the markets. Highly liquid means that a security is easily bought and sold.

Long Bond   The 30-year U.S. Treasury bond is the longest maturity for a bond issued by the government. It is also the most widely traded bond in the world. It is viewed as a benchmark in the industry and is commonly referred to as the "long bond."

Maturity (or Maturity Date)   The maturity date is when the face amount of a security is returned to the investor. A bond issue can have multiple maturities.

Money Market Fund   A fund designed for the short-term storing of cash. Securities and other instruments used in the money markets include federal funds, certificates of deposit, repurchase agreements, Treasury bills, commercial paper, and bankers acceptances.

Municipal Securities Rulemaking Board (MSRB)   The self-regulatory body of the municipal securities markets.

Mutual Fund   A pool of investment capital from people who share the same investment goals. Mutual funds made up of bonds do not have a fixed maturity date. As a bond matures, the funds are reinvested. This removes the hold-to-maturity safety feature from the bonds in an open-end mutual fund.

New Issue Market (Primary Market)   A bond offering sold for the first time: also called the *primary offering.*

Noncallable Bond   A bond that cannot be redeemed prior to its stated maturity.

Notes A security similar to a bond but with a shorter term, usually five-year securities. Municipal notes often are secured by specific sources of future revenues, such as tax receipts or bond proceeds.

Offering Date The offering date is the date on which a new offering of stocks or bonds will be available to the public.

Offering Price In the case of bonds, the price and corresponding yield at which an underwriter of securities offers them to investors.

Official Statement A document prepared by an issuer of municipal securities that gives details of the security and financial information for an issue. Much like a prospectus for stocks.

Original Issue Discount A bond offered at a dollar price less than par (100%) which qualifies for special treatment under federal tax law. For tax-exempt municipal bonds, the difference between the issue price and par is treated as tax-exempt income rather than as a capital gain, if the bonds are held to maturity.

Par Value The face value amount of a bond or note, which is payable at maturity. The par value is the amount on which interest payments are calculated.

Pass-Through Securities representing interests in pools of assets, for example, pools of mortgages. The interest and the principal payments on the underlying collateral are "passed through" to the security holders.

Paying Agent The paying agent pays principal and interest for an issuer. Paying agents are usually banks or other designated offices of the issuer.

Preliminary Official Statement The document prepared by or for a municipal securities issuer that gives in detail the security and financial information about the issue.

Prepayment The payment of principal on a debt before it is due.

Premium The premium is the amount by which a bond sells above its par (face) value.

Price Bonds are quoted either in terms of a percentage of par (face) value (98 bid/99 offered) or in terms of yield to maturity (7.25% bid/7.50% offered).

Price to Call Price to call is the price of the bond, expressed as a percentage, to the call date and at the call price.

Primary Market The primary market is the market in which newly issued securities are sold. It includes the auction market for government bonds and the underwriting period for bonds that an underwriter purchases for resale to investors.

Principal The face amount, or par value, of a bond or other debt security.

Put Bond A bond that allows the holder to "put," or redeem, a bond for return of principal. It is virtually the opposite of a call and is used to make the bonds more attractive to investors.

Rating   Ratings are designations given by professional agency services to bonds to indicate the relative credit quality and the ability to pay interest and principal.

Redemption   The paying off or buying back of a bond by the issuer.

Refunding Bond   The replacement of a bond issue with a new issue. Usually a new bond issue will refund an outstanding issue to achieve conditions favorable to the issuer, such as a lower interest rate.

Registered Bond   A form of ownership of a bond whereby the name of the owner as to principal and interest is recorded on the bond certificates and on the books of the corporation or its agent. A registered bond can be transferred only by endorsement of the registered owner or its agent. In the U.S., registered bonds are replacing bearer bonds.

Repurchase Agreement   Also called repos or RPs, these are agreements between buyers and sellers of securities whereby the seller agrees to repurchase the securities at a stated price and stated time.

Revenue Bond   A municipal bond secured and repaid only from a specified stream of nontax revenues is called a *revenue bond*. Examples of revenues include tolls, utility charges, and use fees from public facilities.

Secondary Market   The market for securities that have been previously offered or sold. It is the market where an individual investor buys and sells securities.

Settlement Date   The settlement date is the date on which the transaction settles and either securities or money is due. For many securities, the settlement day is usually the trade date plus three days (T+3).

Sinking Fund Bond   Issuers of bonds are sometimes required to deposit money into a "sinking fund" with a trustee. The money is to be used to redeem a bond prior to its stated maturity date or to repay principal at maturity. This term usually applies to corporate bonds.

STRIPS   Acronym for Separate Trading of Registered Interest and Principal of Securities, the U.S. Treasury zero-coupon program. STRIPS are bought at a deep discount and redeem for their full face value at maturity. They are essentially zero-coupon bonds.

Swap   The sale of a bond or block of bonds and the purchase of another of similar or nearly similar market value. Swaps can be done to achieve different goals, including establishing a tax loss, upgrading credit quality, or extending or shortening the time to maturity.

Taxable Equivalent Yield   The interest rate that must be received on a taxable security to provide the holder with the same after-tax return as the yield earned on a tax-exempt (municipal) security.

Taxable Bond Fund   Mutual funds that invest primarily in corporate bonds to provide a high level of current income.

Tax-Free Bond Fund   Mutual funds investing primarily in municipal bonds to provide tax-exempt income. Such mutual funds are available in state-specific and national munis.

Total Return   Return on investment, with capital appreciation, dividends or interest. The total return is usually adjusted for present value and expressed on an annual basis.

Treasury Bills (T-Bills)   A T-bill is a U.S. government security with a maturity of one year or less. T-bills are purchased at a discount to the full face value, and the investor receives the full value when they mature. The difference, or "discount," is the interest earned. T-bills are issued in denominations of $1000 (formerly $10,000).

Treasury Notes   U.S. government obligations that are available for terms of from 1 to 10 years. Interest is paid twice a year and they can be purchased in denominations of $1000.

Treasury Bonds   Long-term obligations of the U.S. Treasury that mature in 10 to 30 years are called bonds. Interest is paid semiannually, and they can be easily purchased in minimum denominations of $1000.

Underwriter   An investment bank or group of banks agreeing to purchase an entire security issue for a specified price, usually for resale to others.

Unit Investment Trust (UIT)   A trust registered with the Securities and Exchange Commission (SEC) that purchases and packages a fixed portfolio of bonds. The units, which represent a fractional, undivided interest in the trust, are then sold to investors. Investors receive periodic interest and upon maturity of the individual bonds, the redemption value.

Variable Rate-Bond   A long-term bond for which the interest rate is adjusted periodically according to a predetermined formula. Variable-rate bonds can adjust the interest rate as often as daily or as infrequently as annually.

When Issued   A bond issue that has been offered for sale but not yet delivered by the issuer is considered to be trading on a "when issued" basis. Also known as "when, as, and if, issued."

Yankee Bond   A dollar-denominated bond of a foreign issuer registered with the SEC and sold in the U.S. In practice, non-dollar-denominated bonds of foreign issuers sold in the U.S. are also included in the Yankee bond category.

Yield   Yield is a general term describing the percentage return on an investment. It can be made more specific with qualifiers such as nominal (coupon) yield, current yield, yield to maturity, yield to call, and yield to average life. It is sometimes called the *rate of return*.

Yield to Call   Yield to Call is the yield on the bond to the call date, at the call price.

Yield to Maturity   A yield concept designed to give an investor the average annual yield on a security. It is based on the assumptions that the security is held by the investor until final maturity and that all interest received is compounded.

Zero-Coupon Bond   Zero-coupon bonds do not pay interest prior to maturity. The investor receives one payment when the bonds mature. However, interest is accrued and compounded semiannually at the original interest rate.

Index

Michael D. Sheimo has extensive experience as a Registered Representative and Registered Options Principal which he gained working as a broker at the full-service retail level for Merrill Lynch and Olde Financial Corporation. He is an internationally recognized expert on the Dow Theory and has had books published in India, Malaysia, and Japan. Since 1989, Mr. Sheimo has published eight investing books, including the critically acclaimed *Dow Theory Redux* and *Stock Market Rules*, a book that investors have been relying on since 1990 (2nd edition now available, McGraw-Hill, 1999). He currently works as an author and independent business consultant in the Minneapolis area.